D0969066

Educational Research by Practitioners

EDUCATIONAL RESEARCH BY PRACTITIONERS

An elementary casebook

William C. Budd
Sam P. Kelly
Western Washington State College

Harper & Row, Publishers
New York, Evanston, and London

CONTENTS

PART TWO: SELF-STUDY EXERCISES
Exercise number/Content

PREFACE

The purposes of this casebook are:

- to provide illustrations of the kind of studies and investigations that teachers and other school personnel—administrators, counselors, curriculum and special education personnel—typically undertake in their schools and districts
- to offer critical commentaries on the need, design, procedures and evaluation of such studies
- to provide the reader with a series of self-study exercises modeled after such studies and investigations

This is not a basic textbook in educational research. It is not intended to provide the student or practitioner with a detailed presentation of research designs and methodology. Instead, it is intended for use with such a source or by itself as an aid to examining and criticizing basic elements of research studies that might be conducted by relatively untrained or inexperienced practitioners.

The cases provided represent potential studies as outlined by practicing teachers, supervisors, special education personnel, and administrators enrolled in an introductory graduate course leading to the M.Ed. degree. Part of this course, which emphasizes a systematic approach to resolving pedagogical problems, requires the student to outline the rudiments of a study he *might* conduct in the school system in which he works, given the skill, time, and assistance necessary for such a venture. The course assumes that the beginning graduate, or advanced undergraduate, student is quite unfamiliar with basic principles and procedures of educational investigation, but that he is increasingly exposed to such activity through journals, school workshops, and curriculum committees. It further assumes that he should examine his own professional activity with the question, "How might I improve my research methods?" The case study approach, well proven in other areas of the curriculum, is a useful one for answering this question.

Like most such courses, this one has as clientele a wide range of educational practitioners in background, experience, and academic specialization (see the end of the book's introduction for descriptive data). The English teacher, the science teacher, the teacher of exceptional children, the counselor, the supervisor, the administrator— all commonly enter graduate study through the doors of such a course, which bears varying names and credits according to the institution offering it. Undergraduates intending to teach frequently encounter such content in their junior or senior years.

The compilers of this casebook are instructors in a course of this kind. The studies presented have been taken from their files. The original content and arrangement of the studies is unchanged, except that the materials have been somewhat abbreviated for ease of presentation and commentary.

The first major section of this casebook contains fifteen cases followed by the editors' commentary and criticism. The next section contains another twelve cases, this time without commentary and criticism. Here the user is expected to analyze and criticize as, of course, he may do with the first fifteen cases prior to reading the commentaries.

A brief selective bibliography at the end of the text provides references for more detailed study of research designs, critical analysis of research, statistical tools, and procedures. Selections are suggested with the intent that practitioners, not advanced educational researchers, will be the readers.

The editors are indebted to their colleagues, especially from the course in which the cases were produced, for their assistance and suggestions.

W.C.B.

S.P.K.

INTRODUCTION

As explained in the Preface, each chapter in this casebook presents a condensed proposal for a possible study. Each was selected because it (1) represents a cross-section of basic research approaches and problems, and (2) exemplifies common errors, oversights, or omissions that students and teachers commit.

The presentation of each study will follow the same format:[1]

A general statement of the problem. The student is required to delineate the specific area of the study and make a general statement of the question under investigation.

A brief statement of the need for the study and an indication of research already done in the area. The student is to demonstrate his acquaintance with the topic under investigation and show what further research is needed.

A statement of the guiding hypothesis. The student states the research hypothesis he will attempt to test in his study. This hypothesis should specify the variables to be studied and the expected relationship (if any) among these variables. If a statistical analysis of data is to be undertaken, the student should convert his research hypothesis into an appropriate statistical hypothesis.

A description of the population and sample. The student is asked to specify the group to whom the results of his study

---

[1] *Definition of terms* and other additional headings are used where necessary.

will apply. He should state how he would select a sample (if any) from this group.

A statement of procedures. The steps used in conducting the study are described. The student should be able to describe the instruments he would use, the methods to be employed in collecting data, and the precautions taken against contaminating data.

A statement of analysis of the data. The method of analyzing the data gathered is described. Some type of statistical test or other form of suitable analysis and verification should be proposed.

A statement of potential findings and consequences. The student is to sketch briefly the potential outcomes of the study and state the significance of these outcomes.

After each study are the editors' comments. They answer the following questions:

Overall comment. What is the general value of the study? Is it an important area to be examined? Have studies of this type and focus been overdone?

Particular comments. Did the researcher give an adequate statement of the problem? Did he establish the need for this study? Did he state a testable hypothesis? Did he specify a population? Did he state all his procedures and were they adequate? Is the type of analysis he proposed appropriate for the data?

Summary comment. What type of study does this exemplify? How appropriate is it to the particular situation? Has the student been realistic in assessing the context in which the study would be conducted? Did the student offer some assurance that he could, in fact, conduct such a study?[2]

Contributors of cases in this volume were graduate students taking their first course toward the master's degree in education. The cases included were chosen, not at random, but specifically, in order to show various types of potential studies proposed by practitioners. The selections represent several levels of work completed—from first drafts to final papers—and varying degrees of feasibility.

These cases demonstrate the stage of research awareness or sophistication of teachers or special school personnel practicing their profession. The population includes:

- more than four hundred students over the past several years
- students who received their undergraduate degree from more than twenty-five different institutions
- students who last were (or are) employed in several dozen school districts in the U.S. and Canada —mostly on the West Coast (most often in the Northwest)[3]
- practitioners who have been in the field for as little as one year or as many as twelve years since the B.A. degree
- practitioners who teach, administer, or counsel at all levels, K–12, public and private schools
- practitioners with such varied majors as mathematics or music, and those with a minor in statistics or even total unfamiliarity with statistics

[2] Cases may be examined in conjunction with or apart from the critical commentaries following each one.

[3] Little difference in ability has been observed by the course instructors between U.S. and Canadian teachers and graduate students in terms of the variables considered here.

- K–12 teachers of the different qualities and backgrounds that are found in most school systems

Certainly the sample described varies in some ways from the population of all teachers, administrators, et al. But it is the editors' contention that the sample does not vary enough to make the cases in this collection atypical, although they may not conform to the hopeful expectations of experienced researchers or the desired standards of professional and academic bodies, and even laymen, that assume educational questions often are susceptible to well-structured research approaches and are so approached. Something indeed is lacking along the line.

Following the first fifteen chapters, in each of which one case is presented and discussed, are a dozen exercises. These follow the same format as the preceding chapters. There is, however, no commentary; the user of the casebook is to provide his own analysis and criticism. The reader may follow the critical approach used by the editors (insofar as it is appropriate to each exercise), may develop his own approach, or may use a model supplied by the instructor. The exercises, which come from the same corpus of materials as do the prior fifteen cases, are intended to provide the reader with a chance to apply his critical faculties and educational experience.

PART ONE: CASES

PART ONE: CLASSIC

METHODS OF TEACHING SPELLING IN GRADES 10–12 AND ATTITUDES OF GRADES 10–12 ENGLISH TEACHERS TOWARD THE TEACHING OF SPELLING —A DESCRIPTIVE STUDY

How does a person teach spelling? What methods are commonly employed? What do teachers think about various approaches and what are their attitudes in general about the teaching of spelling? These are the questions with which this first case is concerned, at a certain level of the curriculum. An old, persistent problem crops up again.

The problem

The investigator, a high school teacher, is concerned with two particular questions: (1) What are the common approaches used by secondary teachers of English in teaching spelling, especially in grades 10–12? (2) What are the attitudes of these teachers toward teaching spelling?

Need for the study

The investigator notes that a prevalent approach has been the "list" method, and that recently a linguistically based program approach is advocated, and that still other approaches are offered and defended by various proponents. But there are not enough studies available to determine what current methods ". . . are actually being used by high school teachers in their periods of spelling instruction; nor have the attitudes of this group of instructors been tested . . . in regard to the teaching of spelling. . . ."

In supporting the need for such a study, the investigator points out that it is taken for granted that spelling instruction as such actually does commonly occur in high school English classes—despite frequent observations to the contrary. Moreover, generalizations are made repeatedly about teachers' attitudes toward spelling and the methods employed, although there may be little basis for such generalizations. Hence the proposed investigation.

Hypotheses

The purposes of the study are to determine (1) what methods of spelling instruction are prevalent in the state's high school English classes, and (2) the attitudes of English teachers in the state in regard to the teaching of spelling. Specifically:

- methods of spelling instruction prevalent in the state's high school English classes are inconsistent with methods shown by research to be most effective
- attitudes of high school teachers toward the teaching of spelling account for ineffective methods being employed

Definition of key terms

- *high school English classes.* Are those offered in grades 10–12 and are exclusive of other related, but optional, courses such as journalism, creative writing, world literature, and the like.
- *spelling instruction.* Refers to any type of instruction, systematic or incidental.

Population

This includes all high schools in the state—i.e., English classes as defined. The selection is justified by the investigator as one easy to handle, and a population somewhat familiar to the investigator. The schools (in which reside the target population of English classes) are subdivided into four groups:

- schools enrolling 1,000 or more students
- schools enrolling 400–999 students
- schools enrolling 150–399 students
- schools enrolling 149 or fewer students

The schools are coded according to size and so that individual schools can be identified both as to school and grade. Then twenty classes in each grade in each group are to be chosen randomly. In all, 240 classes will be selected.

		Grade		
		10	11	12
Group (by size of school population)	1	20	20	20
	2	20	20	20
	3	20	20	20
	4	20	20	20
		80	80	80

Procedures

A questionnaire will be sent to the chairman of the English Department in each school selected, then by the chairman to the teacher of the particular English class chosen for the sample. If there is more than one teacher of English at a given grade level (as most often would be the case), the chairman will be asked to ". . . flip a coin to determine which teacher will fill out the questionnaire."

The mailing would include, among other elements:

- a letter of introduction (of the investigator)
- a description of the study and its nature
- a statement dealing with ". . . the school's curriculum and what it has to say about spelling relative to the study"

- a section dealing with methods employed by the teacher in teaching spelling
- a self-addressed, stamped, return envelope

No sample questions or further descriptions are provided. It is noted that an effort has been made to make the answering of questions uncomplicated and not time-consuming; circling or underlining or ranking is to accomplish this.

Analysis of data

Chi-square analysis is proposed as the best method for analyzing the relationships sought. These relationships consist of:

- method and attitude of teacher
- method and size of school
- method and grade level (10, 11, or 12)
- method and sex of teacher
- method and level of educational attainment of teacher

Further discussion concerns the necessity of subdividing attitude and method into specific categories so that the announced relationships will have meaning.

Potential findings and consequences

Here are mentioned the opening up of further studies, the possibility of discovering that methods used in teaching spelling are not those found most productive, the finding that many students in grades 10–12 receive very little or no spelling instruction, and the possible finding that spelling instruction ranks low on curricular priority listings.

In conclusion, the following likely sources of error were mentioned:

- inadequate return (under 50 percent) of questionnaires, or nonproductive returns

- ambiguity of items (pretesting mentioned as a guard here)
- the possible influence on methods or attitudes of a specific required course of study in a curriculum guide

COMMENTS

The reader may wonder why such an "un-study" is included as the initial case in this collection. The answer is that it offers, in linear form (point by point), an opportunity to comment both on the development of design and on some characteristic perils (here quite extreme) of the very common survey approach to the answering of an educational question. Subsequent cases, more deserving of the title "investigation," provide specific examples of weakness in design or procedure. This case offers more of a feast (although it should be added that this study is not unique—an evening spent in combing various journals would scratch up some near acquaintances).

Positively speaking, the aims of the investigator seem worthy. Much attention to spelling and to investigations of spelling have left the investigator's questions at least partially unanswered, even though his questions are concerned with "what" and not with "why." An initial qualification needs to be made before any additional commentary is offered: The investigator assumes there are "known successful methods" of teaching spelling. This assumption undergirds this study, but incontrovertible evidence for this is lacking.

The first weakness of this study concerns the problem of attempting to attack two questions at once: methods of teaching spelling and attitudes of teachers toward the teaching of spelling. The former would seem to call for categorizing methods according to predetermined categories (approach, emphasis, content, whatever). The second would demand a far more difficult categorization: attitudes (an undefined term in this putative investigation). Could a single questionnaire do the job, even if logical and discrete categories were formulated? One thing at a time—at least at this investigator's stage.

Second, in discussing the need for his proposed study the investigator emphasizes only *his* observations regarding the incidence of spelling instruction in grades 10–12, and the methods employed. Personal observation is acceptable when substantiated. One would assume, however, that the literature on spelling research would help confirm or deny the extent of what he observed. A day or less in the proper section of an appropriate library or curriculum shop should suffice. Impressions of colleagues would be helpful, too.

Hypotheses should help direct a study. Here they do this somewhat, but the investigator is still left with a shotgun, not a rifle. In his definition of terms he overlooks such key words as *attitudes* (what? how described?), *methods, ineffective* (by what criteria?), and so on. How then can a questionnaire be developed? Will it produce any coherent, consistent information? How will the investigator sort and categorize, then analyze, his information?

The population appears to be adequate. Certainly a state provides enough of a range of schools and classes to allow for cross-sectioning variations to blend into the information sought without slanting the results. But one particular question is raised: what about the numbers of teachers and classes in the four groupings of schools? While he chose twenty schools randomly (for each grade 10–12), is the investigator providing equal chance for both "big city" teachers and other teachers to be selected? This might not be important if his purpose were not as announced (although method and size of school is one of the data analyses he mentions). If, however, methods and attitudes in general (not by school population size) are sought, there is a problem. Why, one wonders, are the schools subdivided at all? The hypotheses advanced are of little illumination here.

One can only speculate what the questionnaire would turn out to be. The investigator's criteria of noncomplexity and ease of response are encouraging. But without hard definitions of key terms, how will he construct questions, and how will he analyze and categorize responses? A statistical test is the least of his worries at this stage.[1]

His questionnaire certainly should be pretested extensively with a sample of his target population (not the particular schools eventually to be used). This should be done after he has spent time in satisfying objections to other key points, and after examining enough questionnaires and textual commentary on questionnaires to realize the difficulties involved in this form of data-gathering.

In turning to the investigator's projected analysis of data, one finds that he now introduces a cluster of relationships not mentioned earlier. And so here is yet another purpose, and a new study, and probably another statistical approach, and . . . if ever the study was on a line, from beginning to end, the line by now has been replaced by a spiral.

[1] The author suggests the use of chi-square in his analysis because his data are compiled from tabulations. He is interested in determining the relationship between method and five other variables taken one at a time. The chi-square "test of independence" will tell him whether these variables are in fact related to each other or whether they are independent of each other. Should the author wish to obtain a numerical estimate of the magnitude of the relationship between the two variables, he can use the value of chi-square that he obtains from his test of independence and calculate a "contingency coefficient" that will give him an approximation of the product-moment relationship between the variables.

Potential findings must remain potential, for they hardly could be considered research findings in this case. The investigator does indicate a few main hazards, some of which have been discussed. Each hazard is uncontrolled, which would deny validity to any potential findings. One important potential source of error not mentioned is the effect on responses, and hence on findings, that teacher personality, opinion, and bias may have on the teaching of spelling and on related notions or attitudes.

Back to the drawing board! This case exposes, in extremity, many of the hazards of the survey, a most common and often most helpful approach to determining *what* (not why) the situation is in regard to some educational issue, practice, condition, or whatever. The reader can develop his own list of additional criticisms and suggestions —for example, given other necessary improvements, would interviews be better devices for obtaining information? In justice to the investigator, it should be added that additional study and effort—and library-digging—produced a single-purpose revision and a redesign that had some intrinsic merit as well as a possibility of extrinsic employment.

A final word: Misuse of the survey possibly alienates more persons than does any other research approach in education. The investigator often destroys potential cooperation for both the present and future moment, for himself and others, by such incomplete or confusing designs and purposes as here outlined.

THE RELATIONSHIP BETWEEN SPELLING ACHIEVEMENT AND A PERSONALITY FACTOR —A DESCRIPTIVE STUDY

This chapter presents and discusses a study proposed by a secondary teacher of language arts. This teacher is interested in determining whether or not performance in spelling, as measured by a standardized instrument, is related to a specific component of personality.

The problem

It is the investigator's purpose to determine the relationship between achievement in spelling and the compulsive component in personality. Specifically, does a high score on the Junior-Senior High School Personality Questionnaire's (HSPQ) Q3 factor correspond to the spelling achievement of tenth-grade students who have about the same general academic aptitude?

Need for the study

Most studies investigating spelling achievement have dealt with either the teacher-student factor or the individual and his approach toward learning to spell. It is known, however, that personality—variously defined—has some relationship to academic success. Yet in the area of spelling investigation, the possible interplay between spelling achievement and personality type, or factors, has been overlooked or minimized relative to other research concentrations. It thus seems important to investigate the degree of relationship, if any, between spelling achievement and a particular personality factor or characteristic. Here the focus is on tenth-grade students, a group that often does not have formal spelling in their curriculum (and a group that was available to the researcher).

Hypothesis

The null hypothesis to be tested is that there is no correlation between the strength of the Q3 factor score and spelling achievement (.05 level of confidence).[1]

Definition of key terms

- *spelling achievement.* Refers to achievement measured by scores received on the Metropolitan Achievement Battery (Form U-V), selected for tenth-grade students.
- *compulsive component of personality.* "A personality pattern characterized by chronic, excessive, or obsessive concern with adherence to standards or conscience or of conformity. The person may be overinhibited, overconscientious, and may have an inordinate capacity for work . . . rigid and lacks a normal capacity for relaxation."
- *HSPQ Q3 factor.* A score that indicates a characteristic or factor on the test in question and indicates a precise, compulsive, etc. personality.

[1] Two terms are introduced here that may need some definition. A "null" hypothesis is a statistical hypothesis. Basically, it asserts that any observed relationship between variables may be attributed to the effects of chance. Only if the null hypothesis can be rejected at a reasonable level of confidence can we assert the positive (research) hypothesis to be tenable.

Correlation is a numerical estimate of the strength of the relationship between variables. The most commonly used "coefficient of correlation" is the so-called product-moment correlation or Pearsonian coefficient, named in honor of its discoverer, Karl Pearson. It is likely that this is the coefficient the study author had in mind.

Population

The population is all tenth-grade students, some 200 in number, in the high school in which the investigator teaches. All students are to be given the spelling achievement test in their English classes. The final group to be studied will be those students in the tenth grade with an IQ score above 84 (although in different parts of the description this score was variously set both at 85 and 89).

Procedures

All tenth-grade students would take the HSPQ in September. The school psychologist would administer the test since he is best qualified to do so. He also would determine which students show a high score on the Q3 factor of the test in their regular English classes. After the spelling tests are graded, the investigator will attempt to determine a relationship between these tests (scores) and the results of the HSPQ, using only those students who had IQ's above the prescribed level.

Treatment of data

If the results show a significant positive correlation between high scores on the HSPQ and on the spelling achievement test, at the .05 level, the null hypothesis will be rejected. A finding of no significant correlation would permit retention of the hypothesis. There would have to be no significant correlation in *either* direction, at the .05 level, for the statistical hypothesis to be retained as tenable.[2]

[2] By a "significant" correlation here, the author means a correlation that differs by more than a chance amount from a postulated "true" population value of zero. It would be possible to obtain some value (say .10) which, although numerically different from zero, still might have occurred through the chance irregularities associated with the sampling process.

Notice also that the author is proposing a "two-tailed" test of

Potential findings and implications

The investigator writes that it is likely ". . . that no significant findings will occur or that negligible results will be the outcome." This would be expected from the many studies of spelling achievement that have resulted in little advancement of knowledge in this whole area. If significant results do occur, they might well be due to variables other than the compulsive factor under discussion. Should significant findings result, additional study would be indicated, but at least a hint will have been provided of a profitable direction to follow.

COMMENTS

This study deals with the relationship, if any, between achievement in spelling and a personality factor that denotes a somewhat compulsive, socially regulated, scrupulous type of person. The target population is tenth-graders of average or above-average intelligence. Standardized tests are to be used in determining the students' IQ, spelling achievement, and personality characteristics.

It should be noted that the tests named rank in order of objectivity and common agreement as to meaning along a continuum, with spelling achievement the most objective and empirical, then IQ, then personality. In other words, there is agreement on orthography—or something approaching agreement—but less agreement by far on what constitutes personality or its measurement. And IQ tests both define and measure IQ. This creates certain obvious problems of verification, meaning, and comparison.

---

significance. In other words, he believes that the final correlation could be *either* positive or negative. If he thought it would *only* be one or the other, he would use a "one-tailed" test.

The introduction to the study points out that personality factors are known to have a direct bearing on students' curricular achievement, but that there has been relatively little investigation linking spelling achievement to personality factors, at least as compared with the large amount of investigation relating spelling achievement to intelligence, motivation, aptitude, and so on. One hardly can disagree with this position, for the yields from investigations in the area of spelling have been fairly unfruitful despite the great amount of research to date. The investigator expresses a common frustration of teachers: Why are otherwise competent and able persons (e.g., high school and college graduates) poor spellers? Compulsiveness presents itself as a reasonable factor (independent variable) to be examined.

The implied hypothesis of the study is that there is a positive relationship between spelling achievement and the score obtained on a component of the HSPQ test—the component being the Q3 score obtained on the test. The stated statistical hypothesis is that there is no significant (.05 in this case) relationship (null hypothesis). The findings are to be expressed in terms of correlations. No variables other than IQ, spelling achievement as measured by a standardized test, and the Q3 score are accounted for or controlled. Hence if such variables do exist their importance is uncontrolled.

The population includes some two hundred tenth-grade students in a particular high school in which the total student enrollment is approximately six hundred. There is no indication as to the social, economic, or cultural composition of the community; although such variables are likely to have a bearing on the outcome of the test (either in terms of spelling achievement or Q3 scores), this is not considered. Generalizations of findings therefore would be possible only if one assumed—or better yet had evidence—that the community and the home environments of the students were fairly standard and representative, or if one assumed that the relationship between spelling achievement and Q3 score is independent of these variables and of still other unnamed variables.

The method of testing and the timing of testing are not wholly clear. Apparently the two hundred students will be given the personality measure by the school psychologist. He will identify those students scoring high on the Q3 component. Then these students, except those with an IQ of less than 84 (or 85–89) will take the spelling test in their regular English classes. Next, correlations will be run to determine the relationship between scores made on the two tests.

Whether or not the two tests are to be given the same day, week, or month is unclear. At best they should be taken closely together to minimize any loss of sample or any variables related to time and consequent growth in skill, or change in personality. Also, it is unclear whether or not all students in the English classes will take the spelling test; one would hope so in order to reduce any effects that might occur from singling out a portion of a group for a special task.

A question should be raised about the scoring of the tests by the school psychologist. Why is he to identify only high scores? It is not clear from the text whether or not the psychologist is truncating the sample at this point in the procedure. If so, why? Another question concerns the elimination of students with low IQ scores. Their number would be small (if 84 is the cutoff point), and the reason for eliminating them rather than maintaining the entire sample is not given. Better yet, the use of the entire sophomore class is desirable, especially if data processing equipment is available. It takes but little time to punch an IBM card, and two hundred cards could be handled easily and at little cost. For that matter, hand tabulation would not be formidable.

In order to gain additional information from the study, it seems desirable to administer both tests to all students, IQ notwithstanding, and to run correlations with all students *and* with top and bottom groups as determined by IQ, Q3, and spelling achievement. Not to do so would leave unanswered certain conceivable questions: for example, how do students with low IQ's do on the spelling test and on the Q3, etc.? Several cross-correlations are possible here, and not to pursue them is to ignore maximum possible output of the design and the information obtained. In passing, it is worth observing that a group of eleventh-graders and one of twelfth-graders would supply considerably more information were they included; and including them would help satisfy questions about differential results in regard to age, learning, maturity, and so on.

In treating the data received, the use of partial correlations seems indicated.[3] For example, if IQ is a complicating factor in terms of the correlation of Q3 and spelling achievement, why not partial out IQ and obtain the direct two-variable correlation? Holding IQ constant in this way would rule out the possible charge that IQ is a controlling factor in results obtained. The little effort needed to do this would make the study tighter and the findings less susceptible to challenge. The statistical test to be employed is the correlation. But the author might better employ another statistical measure—for example, a z-test—in treating the data and running the correlations.[4]

[3] A partial correlation is a type of correlation coefficient employed where we have established interrelationships among three variables, say X, Y, and Z. The assumption is that X and Y may appear to be related because both are related to Z, and it is this "commonality" that provides the basis for the observed relationship between X and Y. What would be the magnitude of the relationship between X and Y if we removed the influence of Z? Partial correlation enables us to answer this question.

[4] A z-test is a test of significance based upon the so-called "normal" distribution. The letter z is the symbol used to designate the so-called "standard measure" or "standard score." Actually, most statistics books have tables giving the size of the coefficient necessary

The outcome of this proposed study would answer a single question: What? It would show what is, in terms of certain relationships. It of course will not tell Why? . . . or How? . . . in terms of factors or forces at work. The value it might have to a classroom teacher is questionable, since no implications for its findings are suggested in terms of classroom teaching, units of spelling, grouping of students, and so on. If it did show a high positive correlation (or a negative one for that matter), better equipped researchers would have to proceed from that point.[5] Nonetheless, a finding of significance would be a step toward additional research.

This is an example of a descriptive study. No variables are controlled except for those related to the testing itself (time, conditions, etc.). The purpose of the study is called prediction. But if it did "predict," the teacher would be left with the questions: What do I do next? Where do I go from here? The answers to these questions lie in the literature with the next echelon of research expertise, for discussion and suggestions. The present researcher could conduct the study as outlined here. Interpretation of findings and improvement of design and control of variables will call for expert assistance. But this does not by itself totally denigrate the value of the study outlined.

---

for significance at the one percent and 5 percent levels for various size samples.

[5] The reason for this injunction is the oft-repeated admonition that correlation does not imply causation. Simply because two things are related to each other does not mean that one is the "cause" of the other. Causation must be demonstrated on other grounds, usually through an experimental study of some sort.

AN OBSERVATION AND ANALYSIS OF THE READING PROGRAM OF SEX-SEGREGATED CLASSES IN THE PRIMARY GRADES —A DESCRIPTIVE STUDY

There is no area in education more thoroughly studied than reading. However, despite a plethora of research studies, much is still unknown. The author of the study in this chapter proposes to investigate an old approach to reading that may have modern relevance—sex-segregated classes. He does not plan to experiment; rather, he plans to observe what actually goes on when classes are segregated by sex.

The problem

It is the purpose of this study to examine a currently oper-ating and successful program of sex segregation in the pri-mary grades in order to describe and analyze (1) the meth-ods used to teach reading, (2) the materials used to teach reading, and (3) the pupil-teacher interaction patterns found in the teaching of reading.

Need for the study

It is a well-established fact that reading difficulties occur much more frequently among boys than among girls. It has long been suggested that sex segregation in the primary grades will tend to offset the initial disadvantage for boys. For the past six years, the primary classes at X Elementary School have been sex-segregated for instructional purposes. In terms of test scores and teacher reactions, the program appears to have been successful. Since this is the case, it would be helpful to know how the instructional program for the boys differs from the program for the girls, if at all.

Population and sample

The sample for this study will consist of grades one, two, and three in X Elementary School. This school is reasonably representative of other schools in the district.

Procedures

The primary device used in describing teaching methods will be a checklist. Observations will be made once every two months by a team of trained testers from a local college. In addition, during May each teacher will be asked to write a description of the reading program in his or her class that year. Ten students will be selected at random from each class in September. All of the written work of these students will be collected and analyzed on the basis of the content skills needed in reading. Tape recordings of a reading lesson will be taken three times in each classroom—in September, January, and May. These tapes will be classified according to type of reading lesson, class, and grade level.

Teaching materials will be described by means of photographs taken in each classroom in September, January, and May. The photographs will be taken from a central location giving four views of the room. A written caption by the teacher will explain the relationship between the photographed materials and the reading program. The collection of student work can also be used to describe materials.

Pupil-teacher interaction patterns will be described using Flander's system of interaction analysis.[1] The scale

[1] Flander's Interaction Analysis is an instrument that enables an observer to classify and quantify the teacher-student and student-student verbal interaction occuring within a classroom.

will be administered in each classroom in December and March by a team of trained testers from the local college.

Analysis of data

The materials collected during the course of the year will be analyzed to determine whether the methods, materials, and interaction patterns for boys' classes differ from those of girls' classes.

Potential findings and consequences

Either boys are taught differently from girls in sex-segregated classes or they are not. If they are taught differently, it would be well to subject sex segregation to experimental test to determine its effect on the reading achievement of the primary pupils.

COMMENTS

This is an example of a study capitalizing on a somewhat novel opportunity open to the researcher. Sex-segregated classes at the primary level are comparatively rare. It may be argued, however, that the author is not making the best use of the opportunity available to him.

Although it does not come through clearly in his statement of the problem, the intent of the author is to determine whether boys are taught differently than girls when teachers have students of only one sex. If they are not, then either the teachers are missing an opportunity or else they feel no need to adjust their approach to account for sex differences.

The school district in the study is located in a relatively large surburb of a large metropolitan area. As such, it would be typical of many other surburban schools. Six classrooms, however, do not constitute a very large sample, especially when they all come from the same school. Nor is it made clear in the discussion just what the population is—from what is the sample drawn?

The statement of procedures is relatively clear. There is some doubt about the checklist to be employed, but presumably a standard form of some sort will be used. No mention is made of validating and testing the checklist before its use. In general, however, what the author plans to do is reasonably explicit.

What he intends to do with his data is unclear, however. At the conclusion of his study he will have the results of checklists; he will have photographs (taken randomly?); he will have recordings; he will have interaction analyses. What will he do with all these? He speaks vaguely of "analyzing" them, but what constitutes analysis in this case?[2] Just how can one tell when boys are being treated differently than girls?

There is no doubt that sex segregation is a *potentially* very useful approach to reading instruction. We have the author's word (and only his word) that it has proved effective in his district. Whether a descriptive study of this sort will help us to decide whether we should all switch to this approach is, at best, doubtful. As outlined, the proposed study hardly would produce findings to serve as the basis for further experimentation.

---

[2] Most likely, chi-square analysis could be used here. The task is to see whether instructional method, materials, and interaction differ according to sex of student. Sex is a dichotomous variable. If the other variables can be categorized in some satisfactory manner, 2×3 or 2×4 tables can be set up and the observations recorded in the appropriate cells. Then a test of independence (described previously in Chapter 1) can be employed.

A STUDY OF BOYS' READING ABILITY IN SEX-SEGREGATED AND COEDUCATIONAL CLASSES AT THE JUNIOR HIGH LEVEL —A QUASI-EXPERIMENTAL STUDY

The previous chapter discussed a descriptive study of sex-segregated reading classes at the primary level. In this chapter the problem is the same, but the approach is an experimental one and the level is junior high school.

The problem

It is the purpose of this study to determine whether developmental reading for eighth-grade boys is better taught in sex-segregated or coeducational classes.

Hypothesis

The hypothesis for this study is that boys of high, moderate, and low reading ability levels will benefit in increased reading growth through participation in sex-segregated classes in the developmental reading section of eighth-grade English.

Population and sample

The population for this study consists of approximately six thousand eighth-grade students in a large, metropolitan school district. These students are enrolled in seventeen secondary schools. Six randomly selected classes from X High School, which employs coeducational classes, will constitute the control group. Six randomly selected classes from Y High School, which employs sex-segregated classes, will constitute the experimental group.

Procedures

The design to be used in this study is a "post-test only" approach. No pretesting will be employed. The test for the dependent variable will be the Gates-McGintie Reading Survey.

Students in question are assigned to one of three ability groups on the basis of their test scores the previous year. There will be two classes within each ability group at each secondary school. Teachers from the English departments of the schools will be randomly assigned to these six classes. In each school the curriculum to be employed will be the Educational Developmental Laboratory's *Listen and Read*, which consists of thirty one-hour taped reading skills lessons.

Analysis of data

The Gates-McGintie Reading Survey will be administered to all twelve classes at the conclusion of the experimental period. Only scores for the boys in the coeducational classes will be used. These scores will be analyzed using a two-way classification of method and ability level. If the t-test between the group means and the subgroup means exceeds the 5 percent level, it can be concluded that the deviations happen beyond the limits of chance.[1] The null hypothesis could then be rejected and the alternative research hypothesis recognized as worthy of further study.

Potential findings and consequences

Comparisons of the post-test data could, in the first instance, lead to the acceptance of the null hypotheses; that is, the

[1] A t-test is a statistical test of significance for the difference between means developed especially for situations where small samples are employed. "Small" is variously defined as somewhere between thirty to fifty or under. The test was developed by an English statistician, William S. Gosset, in 1908.

results may show that there is no significant difference to be found in the reading gains between the two groups and that either method is equally and educationally profitable. On the other hand, it is to be expected that the null hypothesis will be rejected in favor of the alternative research hypothesis; that is, that boys will achieve more reading growth when grouped in sex-segregated as opposed to coeducational classes. It may also be possible to indicate special instructional groupings for classes that are composed of students of high, medium, or low reading achievement. If the research hypothesis is accepted, then sex-segregated classes in developmental reading would demand priority action within the local school system.

COMMENTS

This study exhibits much of the lack of precision in language that is a common phenomenon among inexperienced researchers. The first example of this can be found by contrasting the statement of the problem with the research hypothesis. The statement of the problem tells us that this study will contrast sex-segregated classes with coeducational classes in the area of developmental reading. This seems a reasonable problem. In stating the research hypothesis, however, the researcher introduces some ambiguities into his language and departs somewhat from the statement of the problem. Note the use of the expression "benefit" with increased reading growth. The word "benefit" is a value word that should not be employed in any statement of an hypothesis. Also, "growth" is not really the dependent variable for the study, since the researcher tells us that he is only using post-test results in his analysis. There is no need to use the three categories of high, medium, and low reading achievement, since presumably these expressions exhaust all possibilities. They may be appropriate to the analysis of variance he proposes to use at the conclusion of the study, but their use is inappropriate here.

The population for the study is misstated. Although there are seventeen secondary schools in this district, the researcher is not making use of all of these schools. He is simply using two of these schools which, for unexplained reasons, happen to be available for the study. Since all of the "experimental" classes are in one school and all of the "control" classes in another, error attributable to differences between schools might well account for any observed difference at the conclusion of the study.

At least two criticisms can be leveled against the experimental procedures. A "post-test only" approach is normally used when subjects can be randomly assigned to treatments *prior to* the study. It is appropriate where pretesting is either not feasible or else might interfere in some unknown way with the final observations. These conditions do not apply here. As a matter of fact, pretest results are available in the form of results of reading tests from the previous year.

The author also fails to specify the length of the experimental period. He does say that the curriculum will consist of thirty one-hour tapes, and so we might infer that the research period will cover thirty instructional days. It is questionable whether thirty days would be sufficient to demonstrate any experimental effect in an ability so resistant to change as reading.

In his analysis the author proposes to use only the scores for the boys from the control group. This means that he will have approximately twice as many scores for his experimental group as for his control group. Moreover, this procedure may introduce disproportionality into his analysis of variance, since in coeducational reading classes we would expect boys to be concentrated in the medium and low categories (as typically occurs).[2] Corrections can be made for such disproportionality in a two-way analysis of variance, but it is unlikely that this researcher would be familiar with the process.

The researcher exhibits his less-than-complete grasp of analysis of variance in his sentence, "If the t-test between the group means and the subgroup means exceeds the 5 percent level, it can be concluded that the deviations happen beyond the limits of chance." In the first place, the analysis of variance utilizes an F-test rather than a t-test.[3] In the second place, it is difficult to determine how or why he differentiates between groups and subgroups. The latter part of the statement exhibits an incomplete grasp of probability theory, since it is difficult to conceive of any experimental event happening "beyond the limits of chance."

The study has many deficiencies. Despite the importance of sex differences in the area of reading, we would hope that no school board would take priority action based on the results of a study so inadequately designed as this one.

[2] This occurs because girls typically score higher than boys on reading tests. Thus if coeducational classes are grouped on the basis of the results from such tests, the proportion of boys in the lowest group will be high. The converse will be true for the highest group.

[3] The F-test is a variance ratio. It was originally devised by the English statistician, Sir Ronald A. Fisher, to determine the significance of the difference between two variances. It is most commonly used in procedures based upon the "analysis of variance," a technique also developed by Sir Ronald. The major advantage of this technique is that it enables us to make simultaneous comparisons among a number of groups.

A COMPARISON OF TWO METHODS OF TEACHING ELEMENTS OF INDUSTRIAL EDUCATION TO A PARTICULAR GROUP OF STUDENTS: THOSE CLASSIFIED AS MENTALLY RETARDED —A QUASI-EXPERIMENTAL STUDY

The teacher proposing this study is interested in determining (1) whether or not mentally retarded students can learn certain skills and contents of vocational education, and (2) if so, which of two approaches would be the more productive: the individual-project method or the mass-production method.

The problem

As between the two stated methods, which is more productive in:

- enabling students to perform certain skills
- enabling students to acquire particular knowledge
- fostering successful interpersonal relationships among the students

Need for the study

The student classified as mentally retarded often is able to acquire sufficient skill and knowledge to pursue a vocation, or at least to perform vocational tasks efficiently and satis-factorily. Because such students typically learn more slowly than do other students, and because the method of learning here is very important, attention needs to be directed toward determining both the type of skill that can be mastered and the most productive approach toward mastery or sufficiency. The literature shows that the individual-project approach and the mass-production approach are both effective to varying degrees.

Evidence also shows that failure of such persons in occupational experience does not necessarily occur only because of low intelligence; it may be fostered by the type of social and vocational setting in which training or application occurs. More needs to be known about both the method and the interrelationship of method and setting.

Hypothesis

The author uses the null hypothesis—that there is no significant difference between the individual-project method and the mass-production method in terms of mentally retarded students' acquiring knowledge, skill, and improved interpersonal relationships.

Definition of key terms

- *method A.*   Involves the teaching of industrial education by the individual-project approach in which the teacher (or student) chooses the project and the student works individually toward its completion.
- *method B.* Involves the mass-production approach whereby the teacher decides on the project, and each student is given a certain portion of the overall project to complete. Periodically the student is changed from one part to another, from planning to assembling to finishing, etc. The student thus gains experience, episodically, with each phase of the project.
- *mentally retarded students.* Include (for this study) persons with IQ's ranging from 50 to 75 as measured by standardized tests, as well as persons with a distinct impairment of adaptive behaviors in day-to-day social performances and situations.

- *skills.* Refer (in this case) to the ability to do things satisfactorily with one's hands or with tools.
- *interpersonal relationships.* Concerns the ability to work well with and to get along with others in a specific situation.

Population

The population is mentally retarded students of (high school) junior age or status (by nonselective promotion) enrolled in a large school system. Students will be males between the ages of fourteen and sixteen years.

The sample consists of six junior classes of mentally retarded boys, two classes in each of three secondary schools. The schools will be chosen randomly from among district secondary schools.[1] Students selected will be assigned randomly to either one or the other of the two instructional situations—individual project or mass production.

Procedures

After assignment, one class will be the control group; the other, the experimental group. The control group will be the individual-project class in each school, since this method is the more common and the more traditional. There will be three classes of each type.

One teacher will instruct both the experimental and the control group in each school. Teachers will be chosen against certain criteria:

- they will be industrial education teachers experienced in teaching mentally retarded students
- they will have taught both approaches or methods
- they will volunteer to participate in the study

[1] *Randomly* means equal opportunity to be chosen from among a described, known population, or to be assigned to one or another treatments or groups.

Through consultation with the participating teachers, the investigator will choose the content (task and knowledge) for the classes. The instructors and investigator will together devise tests appropriate to the content. During the period of instruction, classes will be given several short, fairly simple, oral objective tests on knowledge (item identification, use, nomenclature, etc.) related to the content. These brief tests will be given to all classes at the same time. The final, more extensive test will emphasize performance.

"The reliability of the final test will be determined by giving it to mentally retarded seniors who have completed the junior class. The split-half method will be used, and the Spearman-Brown formula will be applied to the test to determine its reliability. The reliability of the test will first be found before it is administered to the experimental and control groups." [2]

At the concluson of the experiment, the teachers will have students in both groups complete certain exercises that demand skills emphasized in the training just completed. A checklist developed by investigator and teachers will be used to evaluate students' performances.

[2] The reliability of a test is the consistency with which it measures. In order for a test to be of any worth, it must be demonstrable that it is measuring something (whatever it might be) consistently.

Where there is only one form of a test, it is customary to demonstrate the reliability by correlating scores from one-half of the test with scores derived from the other half of the test. The usual procedure is to score the odd-numbered items and then the even-numbered items. Unfortunately, this procedure tends to reduce the magnitude of the reliability coefficient thus calculated because the length of the test is decreased by 50 percent. A longer test tends to be a more reliable test. To compensate for the decrease in length of the test, the Spearman-Brown formula is used to estimate what the reliability of the test would be were it restored to its original length.

Through consultation with counselors and teachers, the investigator will prepare a list of criteria for rating interpersonal relations (e.g., cooperation and hostility) among the students in both groups. The school counselor in each participating school will observe both groups within his school and will do so often enough to observe each student individually six separate times. In doing this he will utilize the checklist just mentioned.

Treatment of data

The means of all scores (quizzes, the longer test, and the final performance task) will be computed for both groups in each school. Then all control group scores will be lumped together, as will all experimental group scores, and a mean will be calculated for the total enrollment of each of the two overall groups. Statistical analysis will tell whether or not the two groups differ significantly. Moreover, the mean scores of the two overall groups in terms of interpersonal relationships, skill, and knowledge will be compared statistically. Thus a total of four scores will be compared (as between control and experimental groups).

It is assumed that several variables are controlled by this method of selection and treatment:

- representativeness of students among schools and among the general population specified
- skills and knowledge students possess at the beginning of the study
- interpersonal variability evened out among groups
- adequacy of observation by evaluators, and commonality of procedure and criteria among teachers and evaluators

The possible peril in using a locally created and administered evaluation checklist is noted.

Potential findings

Acceptance of the null hypothesis would indicate no significant difference among methods. If this occurs, the choice of method would be determined by such factors as ease, individual instructor's preference, cost, and so on. If one method is shown to be more effective than the other, that method would be suggested as the one to be adopted in the district wherever feasible, or the one to be compared to yet another possible approach. Should one method show gain in one area—say skill—but loss (comparatively) in another—say interpersonal relationships—a value judgment would have to be made by the instructor, the principal, or some other authority in choosing Method A or Method B.

COMMENTS

This study seems pertinent and socially valuable. Retarded students need every advantage that can be mobilized to assist them. If a certain method of instruction can help them better accomplish desirable tasks, then that method demands trial and testing. No doubt research findings exist that bear upon the investigator's study, but apparently for his school system the investigation is potentially fruitful, and perhaps for a larger audience as well.

But there are questions to be raised and criticism to be advanced. First, the time involved. How long a period would be devoted to the content proposed for the two groups? The investigator is not specific. Would a month be long enough? Would a term be better? With the students he has in mind, an elaborate project would not seem indicated; yet in order to make evaluation meaningful, a period of at least some weeks would seem minimum. Then, too, mastery of a skill may come readily, mastery of a certain amount of knowledge equally readily; but a significant change in interpersonal relationships argues for a longer period of time. Such change in relationships, if any, should be checked in other settings than just a single class to see if the change is a localized phenomenon or a more extensive adjustment. Would it persist? Moreover, why not check at the beginning for the degree of interpersonal relationship as well as during the study?

The definition of groups is not clear. How many students would be in control classes; how many in experimental classes? The mass-production technique seems potentially more serviceable with large groups than does the individual-project method, which likely would need more instructional supervision, consultation, and perhaps more facilities. Inherent in the design are possibilities for using different size groups while retaining the ability to make valid cross-comparisons, thus somewhat satisfying questions about "best size." (However, this was not a query posed by the investigator.)

The range of IQ, while perhaps standard by definition of "retarded," is an element to consider. Can IQ 50 compete with IQ 75? The study apparently makes no provisions for subcategorizing students to determine more exactly who might prosper under which method. It is conceivable that Method A could prove productive with the low range of IQ's and Method B with the higher range, or vice versa. Group means may not show this clearly. It would not be difficult to determine this by a bit more effort and analysis, and the results might be instructive.[3]

[3] The usual method of doing this is to employ what are known as "factorial" designs. The major advantage of a factorial design is that it enables determination of whether any "interaction" effects occur among the variables used in the study. In this particular study there could conceivably be an interaction effect between method and level of intelligence.

One should beware of easy categorizing. Mentally retarded students may well vary, as do other students, in such matters as interpersonal relationships, according to variables such as number of siblings, home environment, family income, and so forth. While the assumption seems to be that such factors even out through random selection, the size of the groups treated is important here as is the initial designation of mentally retarded. Not all students scoring IQ 75, for example, end up in classes for the mentally retarded. Although the present investigator has little control over this, he should be aware of such likely factors and should consider them.

The number of control and experimental groups seems adequate and the selection processes suitable, or at least as much so as ordinarily could be arranged in the schools. A critical factor is the separation of the two methods. In one method the student proceeds by himself through the completion of a project, apparently step by step. In the other method he is moved from element to element as the overall project is accomplished by the group. But does the "mass" student benefit from the visibility of the various elements as they are undertaken in the same setting in which he is working? Or does the mass technique occur step by step but with most students taking the same step apace? If the latter, how in essence does it differ from the individual approach except for possible rate of progress? This point is not clear, but it is a factor that needs explanation. Also needing clarification is the degree of cooperation involved in the mass approach, since one would assume, *a priori*, that this element would abet improved interpersonal relationships by its very nature. The point is that the investigator must understand very thoroughly the differences that exist in the operation and structure of the two methods so that he is not assuming differences that do not exist in practice. A finding of no significant difference may indicate only that the two methods are similar in most details, or emphasis, or opportunity—not that two different methods are equally productive or unproductive.

The testing and quizzing seem appropriate and their composition valid—reflective of the aims and content—insofar as they are described here. The dangers of a teacher-made test in which one of the parties is also the experimenter are partly controlled by the inclusion of other parties involved in the study. Nor is the investigator relying solely on his skills; he intends to involve school counselors in constructing and evaluating checklists for the interpersonal element of his study. The overall mean score and the submean scores provide general and specific data, except that, as noted, the range of IQ's is great.

Still another matter involves the acceptance or rejection of the null hypothesis. At what level is it to be rejected? The .05 or even the .10 level would seem indicated, not the .01 level. The study and its terms and comparisons do not seem defined enough to aim for .01 confidence; nor would such certainty be necessary. To make the announced comparisons of means, adequate statistical devices are available, assuming that the classes are of sufficient size (not restricted to a very few students in each group).

The variables noted by the investigator indicate that he has a fair idea of some of the hazards of his proposed study. Others have been discussed here, and still others could be identified: for example, the perils inherent in using a volunteer teacher group (who volunteers? why?). This is an example of a meaningful, school-centered, semi-experimental study. *Semi-* because it does not offer the controls, precision, and isolation of key variable(s) for manipulation that would qualify it as a true experiment in the more controlled or clinical sense of the term. Its value is inherent in its clientele, and its likelihood of producing meaningful results—with necessary revisions—is such as to encourage its attempt. By applying this type of approach to education, more teachers and administrators would improve their critical abilities, their curriculum, and most importantly the progress of their students. This study illustrates the kind of educational question that is quite susceptible to inquiry by classroom teachers and school administrators.

THE EFFECT OF TIME OF DAY UPON THE PERFORMANCE OF ELEMENTARY SCHOOL STUDENTS IN ARITHMETIC —A QUASI-EXPERIMENTAL STUDY

This is a study proposed by an assistant principal of an elementary school. In assigning periods for certain types of academic work in the upper elementary grades, he has had teachers object when their arithmetic classes were scheduled for the afternoon. He proposes to find out whether or not it really makes any difference in achievement if arithmetic is taught in the morning or in the afternoon.

The problem

The purpose of this study is to determine if the performance of arithmetic students in grades four through seven in X Elementary School will be higher in morning or afternoon classes.

Hypothesis

The hypothesis for this study is that there will be no significant difference between the performance scores of students in morning arithmetic classes and their performance scores in afternoon classes.

Population and sample

The population for this study will consist of all students in grades four through seven in X Elementary School. From this population, four classes will be randomly selected to form a sample of approximately 130 students.

Procedures

The timetable at *X* Elementary School is based on a six-day cycle. There are seven forty-minute periods in the day, four in the morning and three in the afternoon. For the purpose of this study, the four experimental classes will be scheduled to be with the homeroom teacher, who teaches all arithmetic, during the first and last periods of the day.

Three times during the year—in October, January, and May—a twelve-day test period will be selected. During these test periods, students in the experimental classes will be taught arithmetic during the first period in the morning (the usual practice) for the first six days of the cycle. For the next six days immediately following, they will be taught arithmetic in the last period of the afternoon. At the end of each six-day period, the students will take a specially prepared test of forty addition problems. There will be a fifteen-minute time limit on the tests. No information concerning the results will be divulged to the students.

From time to time during the course of the experiment, observations will be made in the experimental classes by professional personnel such as the counselor and curriculum consultant. Each person making such an observation will be supplied with a checklist on which he is to record the number of times he observes certain behaviors of both students and teachers. The behaviors to be observed are these:

- **For students**
  looking out window
  talking to another student
  restless moments
  shuffling feet
  daydreaming
  yawning
  bored facial expressions
  vocal expressions of disinterest

- **For teachers**
  irritability
  sitting
  lack of enthusiasm
  indifferent manner of presentation

Analysis of data

At the conclusion of the study, test results (error scores) will be pooled for morning and afternoon classes and the t-test employed to determine whether a significant difference (10 percent level) exists between the two means. Chi-square will be applied to the results from the checklists to determine whether the behavior observed in the morning classes differs from that observed in the afternoon classes. Again the 10 percent confidence level will be employed.[1]

Potential findings and consequences

If the null hypothesis is retained, arithmetic can be scheduled in the afternoon with reasonable assurance that performance will not be adversely affected. If the null hypothesis is rejected, arithmetic should be scheduled for that time which yields the better performance.

COMMENTS

This study tackles a single but irritating problem: Does time of day have anything to do with the amount learned? Unfor-

[1] The researcher has decided here to use the 10 percent level. The particular level of significance to be used for a study is the choice of the researcher. He decides on the basis of the relative importance he attaches to errors of the first kind (rejecting the null hypothesis when we should accept it) as opposed to errors of the second kind (accepting the null hypothesis when we should reject it).

tunately, the researcher complicates his approach somewhat and leaves us in doubt regarding the validity of his findings.

The statement of the problem and the hypothesis are clear enough. The author uses the null hypothesis for his guiding hypothesis, and in this case this is probably appropriate since he will in all likelihood feel satisfied if the null hypothesis is held tenable. If so, time of day apparently makes little difference, and scheduling can be expanded accordingly.

He selects his sample not directly from the population he specifies but from intact classroom groups. The random sample is a sample of classroom units and not of students. This need not necessarily introduce any additional error into his findings, but the logic of the sampling process should be made clearer.

Without a fairly complete pretest given to the control and experimental groups, the question of differential input by sex is raised. Might it be that any differences noted as outcomes could be accounted for by a higher degree of knowledge or ability in arithmetic by, say, boys—who usually score higher in math than do girls? The composition by sex of the classes involved in the experiment might thus have a strong, *independent* effect on outcome. More detailed analysis of findings could determine this.

The experimental procedure is essentially an equivalent-time sampling procedure with a single group. However, the researcher has made no provisions for randomizing the order of the treatments. In each case, arithmetic is taught in the morning for six days and then in the afternoon for six days. With four classes participating, it would be possible for the experimenter to randomize the order of treatment. A serious question can be raised concerning the length of time allowed for the experimental treatment. Will six days be sufficiently long to demonstrate any possible results?

In addition, two other possible sources of error are not controlled. The experimenter states that the usual practice is to teach arithmetic first period in the morning. Thus might it not seem unusual to the students to switch to last period instruction for three six-day periods during the year? Is it not also possible that, as the research suggests, teachers may not put forth their best efforts during the afternoon sessions since they would obviously know the reason for the experiment.

The experimenter would have been well advised to limit his measurements on the dependent variable to his forty-problem addition tests. Such tests have the obvious advantages of clearly apparent relevance and likely high reliability. The checklist has no such advantages. Apparently the experimenter felt there were additional factors besides simple achievement that should be taken into account. Perhaps this is so, but it would be preferable to do so as part of another study. For that matter, even his list of behaviors is not so operational as it might seem. Exactly how can one be certain when a student is daydreaming?

The experimenter encounters the same difficulties in his analysis of data. The t-test applied to the error scores seems straightforward enough. The proposed chi-square analysis of the data from the checklist may not give him the information he wants. Chi-square will tell whether the checks in the morning classes are distributed in the same way as the checks in the afternoon classes. It will not tell, however, whether there is a significant difference in the absolute frequency of the occurrence of such behavior.[2]

[2]In other words, undesirable behavior could occur more frequently in the morning than in the afternoon classes (or vice versa) but if it always distributed proportionately in the categories selected for observation, chi-square would show no significant difference between the groups. To remedy this situation, he would need some observations on "positive" behavior.

Since all of the behaviors listed are negative ones, the only confirmation possible with chi-square is a reshuffling of afflictions.

Since acceptance of the null hypothesis is, in fact, a positive outcome for the experimenter, it is likely that some teachers will be teaching arithmetic in the afternoon in subsequent years.

AN INVESTIGATION OF THE RELATIONSHIP BETWEEN CRITICAL-THINKING SKILLS AND WRITTEN COMPOSITION —A QUASI-EXPERIMENTAL STUDY

This is a study proposed by a high school teacher of English concerned with the perennial problem of teaching students how to write. Presumptively, the key to better writing is better thinking (and the proposed study rests on this *assumed* transfer and similarity of skills).

The problem

It is the purpose of this study to examine the relationship between the direct teaching of certain selected critical-thinking skills and improvement in written composition. The questions asked are: (1) Will students who receive special instruction in certain critical-thinking skills improve more significantly in overall writing ability than students who write an equal amount but who do not receive this special instruction? (2) Does the teaching of critical-thinking skills bring about improvement in any of the criterion areas of writing? (3) Does transfer of training take place with this type of instruction?

Need for the study

High school and college teachers claim that students do not write as well as they should. Attempts to improve student writing have concentrated on such things as grammar, logic, usage, paragraph development, rhetoric, and increases in the quantity of writing. To date, no approach has produced conclusive evidence of results. Some claim that writers are born, not made. Assuming, however, that writing can be taught, a concentration upon critical thinking may help produce better writing.

Hypothesis

The hypothesis for this study is that students who receive special instruction in certain selected critical-thinking skills will improve significantly more in writing ability as judged by student themes than students who write but who do not receive this instruction. The (statistical) null hypothesis will be rejected at a probability level of .05.

Population and sample

The population for the study will consist of eleventh-grade students at X High School. Four classes of such students enrolled in eleventh-grade English will constitute the sample. The classes are to be selected at random from the "average" sections of eleventh-grade English.

Procedures

The four classes in the sample will be randomly designated as two experimental and two control groups. Four teachers from the English department will be randomly assigned to the classes. The teachers will be trained in or oriented to the special method of instruction.

The control groups will (1) read the American literature curriculum contents used in the eleventh-grade in this school, (2) discuss this literature in class, and (3) write papers on topics arising from study of the literature. The students' papers will be given thorough evaluation and returned. Sample papers will be reproduced and discussed in class. Students will revise their papers and return them to the teacher, who will provide a final evaluation and grade.

For the experimental groups, one class day a week will be devoted to the teaching of selected critical-thinking skills. Class discussion on other days will emphasize these skills as applied to the literature. In discussing sample papers in class, students will be encouraged to employ such skills. For both groups, the content (literature) will be the same.

Both experimental and control students will write eight papers during the semester. Papers will be from 250–500 words in length and will be written in class. The papers will be spaced throughout the semester, but the groups will not necessarily write at the same time on the same subjects. Some revision of papers may be done outside class.

During the second week of the fall semester, all students will write an in-class paper on the topic "The Role of Student Government in This High School." The following day the students will be asked to write another paper on the topic "One Rule in This School Which I Feel is Unfair— A Proposal to Change or Eliminate It." These papers will be approximately 250 words in length.

Three qualified readers (judges) from outside the district will be used. The papers will be typed by a secretary, errors and all, before they are presented to the readers. (Thus physical appearance will be controlled.) Papers will be identified only by number. The readers will be specially trained in the use of the rating scale to be used; this will be a six-point scale using fifteen criteria. All three readers will record independent ratings for each paper. The papers from experimental and control students will be randomly distributed for judging. The score for each paper will be the sum of the three reader scores.

The first week of the second semester, the students will write two more in-class papers on consecutive days on topics selected by the investigator. These topics, however, will not be about any particular piece of literature. These papers will be read and scored in the same manner as the initial papers.

Analysis of data

It is hoped that the pretest papers will show that the groups selected will be equal for all practical purposes. If this is the case, the final analysis will consider only the post-test results using the "t" test between groups. If the groups are not initially equal, then improvement within the groups must be considered by comparing differences between pre-tests and post-tests. The null hypothesis, that there will be no significant difference in the improvement of the writing of students in experimental and control groups, will be rejected or accepted at the .05 level.

COMMENTS

Certainly the matter of student writing is a pressing problem. Most approaches to the problem have produced little usable information. Perhaps the author of this proposed study is correct in assuming that training in critical thinking will help, although she does tend to underestimate the amount of research already done in this area.

The author poses a three-pronged problem (see "The problem"). Most likely, only the first question is essential to the study. The "criterion areas" mentioned in the second question refer to the fifteen criteria of the rating scale employed. To analyze in such detail (or so divide and categorize) would be beyond the scope of a study such as this one. The question of transfer posed by the third question is either ambiguous or redundant. The study is not a study on transfer in the ordinary use of the word. As the author uses the word in this study, it adds nothing to what was asked in the first question.

The use of the word "improve" in the hypothesis poses certain difficulties. It is, of course, possible to analyze gain scores, but that is not the usual approach to a study of this type. The analysis the author proposes would not demonstrate whether either group had "improved" from pretest to post-test. Other key terms—e.g., "criterion areas of writing"—also are undefined. Thus one cannot be sure that the proposed tests and assignments meet these critical definitions.

The author is using intact groups for a sample. This frequently must be the case in on-the-spot educational research. She does, however, introduce randomization where possible, and this is beneficial to the design in that it helps control for systematic bias.

The procedures seem a bit grandiose for this type of study. Would it really be possible to get school secretaries to type four hundred test papers? Could one really inveigle three other teachers of English from some other district to read the papers? Many appropriate procedures are present—two papers for writer reliability, three readings for reader reliability, numerical coding of papers, etc.—but they have a somewhat hollow ring. One probably would need a research grant to do all this, and the author is not apt to have one.

The researcher seems to have only a hazy idea of the appropriate type of statistical analysis for this study. Undoubtedly, she would need special help for this. Even with three independent readings, the reliability of the post-test scores will likely not be very high.[1] A good guess might be .70. With low reliability, it would be very difficult to demonstrate significant results, so the .05 level seems stringent for such a subjective scoring procedure. Certainly the .10 level might be employed here, with attention to appropriate statistical treatment.

[1] It is difficult to achieve high reader reliability on written material without a great deal of time, effort, and training of readers. By contrast, the reliability of a well-standardized objective test tends to be high, in the neighborhood of .90.

A real stumbling block may be the minor, or totally lacking, difference between control and experimental groups in the independent variable: critical thinking. Is the researcher certain that the experimental groups *only* will have a high measure of this emphasis? Might not this factor be common in literature classes where, by definition, literary criticism of some sort should occur? The researcher states no method for determining how real the difference in this variable will be; it may be different only in label, and observation of typical literature classes from which the study's sample is drawn would help determine this. So might advance discussion with participating teachers.

This study appears to be beyond the depth of the proposer. It has many aspects of good experimental design, but it does not really seem feasible in the typical high-school setting. A more experienced researcher is needed as a partner for such an effort.

Case eight

THE INFLUENCE OF MUSICAL STIMULI ON THE RHYTHMIC PATTERNS IN PAINTINGS OF TENTH-GRADE STUDENTS —A QUASI-EXPERIMENTAL STUDY

This investigator, an art teacher, is interested in determining the possible influence of a certain pattern of music on the organization of student paintings.

The problem

Will there be a notable difference in the number of rhythmically organized paintings of tenth-grade students where musical stimulation is used?

Need for the study

"The use to which the student puts the creative process in the art class is unique among his other classes . . . the time allotted to art is meager . . . it is necessary (therefore) to find some method which will help the *beginning general art student* relate to the individual-centered environment generally encountered in an art activity class. The process of making art, or . . . creating and building artistic forms, is often an informal, illogical, and messy-looking affair. However, . . . through such a process . . . the subjective happenings inside the student are brought forth. To provide a familiar note in the art environment, the use (of a particular pattern or type) of music may be helpful."

The investigator notes that the use of music in the classroom is not new. But research, it is claimed, has not made any final conclusions about effectiveness or about functional and sensory processes as they relate to artistic performance.

Hypothesis

The hypothesis employed is the null hypothesis (.10 confidence level using a two-tailed test): that there will be no measurable difference in the number of paintings organized rhythmically where rhythmic musical stimulation is used as compared with the number of paintings organized (or not organized) rhythmically in classes not employing music.

Definition of key terms

- *rhythmic pattern.* The pattern the drawing imposes on observed facts (i.e., rhythm).
- *carefully selected music.* Refers to strongly rhythmic selections suitable to the age group and the purpose of the study. The selections would be made by a committee including chairmen of high school music departments and a college professor from a department of music. The selections would be presented on twenty-minute tapes, each including different selections but all selections equally (by decision) rhythmic.
- *beginning general art students.* Include a cross-section of tenth-grade students typically having little or no experience with the subject.
- *art teachers.* Those teachers with the B.A. who teach art, who have at least three years of teaching experience in the subject, and who majored in art.
- *art judges.* Public school and university art teachers and the owner of an art gallery.

Population and sample

The population consists of all future general art students in the school system in which the study will be conducted, plus students in like systems and at the same grade level. The sample will be four intact groups (students assigned to the classes) of first-semester general art students in two large high schools in the school district. Each of the schools normally offers two such art classes the first semester of the school year.

Procedures

With permission from the superintendent of schools, the following procedures will take place. One teacher of art within each school will be selected randomly to teach both classes in the high school (assumedly all the teachers meet the qualifications listed in "Definition of Key Terms"). One of the two intact groups in each school will be selected randomly as the experimental group; the other group will serve as the control group. Groups will average about twenty-five students.

The control and experimental groups will receive similar instruction taken from the syllabus commonly used in this course. Beginning the third week of the term, the experimental groups will be exposed twice weekly—at random times—to a variety of music (not just rhythmic selections). This will be done to accustom these students to the background presence of music and, hopefully, will reduce the "Hawthorne" (conscious and visible) effect of such an intrusion.

Later in the term, the experimental treatment will be introduced concurrently with a unit on watercolor and tempera paints and painting. This procedure will start the seventh week of the term and last three weeks. At the time of the experimental treatment, each teacher will be provided with a set of identical musical tapes. Tapes will be numbered from one to six. On six randomly selected days during the three-week experimental period and unit, teachers will play the six twenty-minute tapes (in both experimental classes). At the time the tapes are played, both experimental sections will discuss and paint the same general themes, as will the two control groups. In all instances, the same days will be used for each action described. The painting time for all groups will be held constant.

The students' work in all four classes will be collected at the end of the period on each of the six days the programmed music is played. These "works" will be coded and numbered, for both the experimental and control classes. A table of random numbers will be employed to select thirty "works" from the control groups and thirty from the experimental groups. The sixty selections will be displayed randomly while they are hung in a large room.

Then the team of judges will independently rate each painting, looking only for the presence or absence (and degree) of rhythmic organization or pattern. Judges will rate each selection by using a three-point scale: 0–2, with 0 indicating no rhythmic pattern and 2 indicating a high degree of rhythmic pattern.

Treatment of data

The four sets (four judges) of scores will be analyzed to determine how the judges agreed in assessment of the variable. Then a composite score will be obtained and the experimental and control groups compared. The difference between means will be calculated and the null hypothesis accepted or rejected. Also determined will be the number of "works" judged rhythmic in each group.

The investigator notes two potential hazards. First, the problem of timing when two schools and four classes are involved. Every effort will be made to control this factor. Second, the problem of agreement on the criterion: degree of rhythmic pattern or composition. This is subjective, although the judges will discuss the criterion and every effort will be made to agree on what is and what is not "rhythmic." However, no standardized definition exists in such an undertaking. (Nor does it exist, except relatively, in selecting Miss America or the winner of the talent show in any artistic or pseudoartistic comparison.)

Potential findings and implications

Rejection or acceptance of the null hypothesis might mean that the music worked, did not work, was inappropriate, or that measurement could not be made precisely enough. Also, if the hypothesis is rejected, more refined studies would be indicated. Do other types or patterns of aural stimuli influence student artistic patterns and composition? Questions also would be raised about giftedness, the degree of musical knowledge or experience the students might have prior to class (do all or some take music lessons?), the degree of involvement in their painting that music provided students, and so on. (Note that the implications also consider uncontrolled variables in the study.)

COMMENTS

This is an interesting and fairly adroit design aimed at trying to uncover the influence of one set of stimuli (aural) on a creation (visual, organizational, tactile) produced by an individual in a particular situation. There are many accounts in the research literature dealing with such overall intentions; but, as the investigator notes, findings are hardly conclusive (does the tempo of supermarket music encourage buying?). Practically speaking, if rhythm, as here defined, is a desirable constituent (or skill) of painting, then the value of the study, and its possible implications, is self-evident. The study provides another example of what classroom teachers can and should do to satisfy their questions and possibly improve their teaching through more precise knowledge than they currently possess.

But there are questions to raise. First, why does the

investigator not propose a trial run using "works" not to be included in the final sample to be judged? Some practice among judges would guarantee a better working definition of what constitutes a "rhythmic" painting. At least, it would acquaint the judges with the type (and degree of talent) of works they are to examine.

Next, is it a particular type of music (rhythmic) or music per se that may influence the degree of rhythmic pattern, if any, found in the efforts of the experimental group? That question remains largely unanswered in the present design. Why not provide one experimental group with a continuation of variable music and the other with "rhythmic" music? Then the question might be better resolved. Also, is there a difference as time passes? That is, would "rhythmic" painting patterns occur early or late as the tapes are played? There might be a plateau factor operating here—noticeable improvement at intervals, not steadily. How long the intervals are, if such is the case, could be critical, since the time might exceed that allowed for the experiment.

One would wish, although this would make the study more complex, that more was known about the students. Would more "rhythmic" pattern appear in the paintings of students who took music lessons? Of those who had high IQ's? Of those who were boys? And so forth. Spot checks could be made in an attempt to gain some insight here so that later studies might have better directions to follow, some likely leads to explore.

This again is out of the present context, but what would be the effects of the same treatment on younger— or older—students?

If the direct purpose of the study is to determine the effect of a certain kind of music on performance in painting or drawing, why does the investigator suggest randomizing his music (the six tapes) as to time of appearance?

One would suppose that more powerful findings would result if the investigator would arrange, by his best judgment, for the music to be introduced at the most propitious time in the unit of study and practice. Her approach seems to be an overdoing of "randomness," which here would not appear to offer any benefit but rather a possible restriction. (Randomness has many uses, but also potential misuses.)

The researcher proposes to test the difference between the mean scores of the two groups. However, the scales he is employing has only three points: 0, 1, and 2. It would take some stretch of the imagination to consider data derived from such a scale as "interval" data; more likely the data are merely ordinal in nature.[1] In this case a median test would seem more appropriate.

Last, one would be reluctant to generalize the findings of the study to the extent the investigator proposes. Without some repetition, the local schools and the students and teachers utilized form the most acceptable limits of generalization.

This is an example of a study that in reality is as much descriptive as it is experimental. True, controls are introduced and an experimental group is employed. But so many conflicting, or unresolved, factors are left uncontrolled or unknown that the question "Does x cause or promote y?" cannot be answered with a certain yes or no. Even so, for what results might occur and for leads to further studies, this provides an example of worthy effort on the part of an inquisitive teacher who wants to seek answers to valid curricular questions rather than suppose the answers.

---

[1] In ordinal data, numbers indicate singly a rank position and nothing more. In interval data, numbers indicate distance in presumably equal units from a known (although arbitrary) zero point.

THE EFFECTS OF GRADING ON ACHIEVEMENT —A QUASI-EXPERIMENTAL STUDY

This chapter presents a study proposed by a high school teacher of English. This teacher is concerned with the Honors English classes taught in his school, and he wonders if in one respect—grading—such classes could be changed with benefit both to teacher and student.

The problem

The purpose of this study is to determine which groups of students enrolled in twelfth-grade Honors English classes will attain the higher degree of scholastic achievement— groups in a "graded" program or groups in a "nongraded" program. Will Honors students achieve more or achieve less when pressure of grades is removed, as compared to similar students working under the assumed pressure of grades?

Need for the study

There are two principal reasons for conducting the study. The first is to challenge the assumed necessity of grades as a factor for motivating achievement. The second is to provide information that may result in local arrangements to help stem the tendency of able students to avoid Honors classes for fear their grade-point average will drop. If it can be demonstrated that achievement will not decline under an arrangement that guarantees a high grade for Honors students, then the study will be considered to have served its purpose.

Hypothesis

The hypothesis is that Honors students in a nongraded Honors English program will advance significantly more, as measured by a suitable achievement test, than will Honors students in a graded program. The statistical hypothesis is that there will be no significant difference in scholastic achievement between the two groups.

Population

The population for his study is all (this district's) high school twelfth-grade Honors students, present and future. The assumption held in specifying this population is that if the criteria for selecting Honors students remain relatively constant, Honors students in subsequent academic years will be much like current Honors students. This assumption occasionally can be checked using data readily available on student permanent record cards, or by the administration of a pretest in English achievement at the beginning of each year.

Procedures

The sample for the study will consist of all Honors students from two consecutive years. There will be approximately sixty students each year. The students for the first academic year will be designated the control group, and the students from the second academic year will be the experimental group. Both the control and experimental groups will be divided into two classes of approximately thirty each by alternate selection from alphabetically arranged registration lists. During the first year of the study, the control groups will be assigned to the same room, one group in the morning and one in the afternoon. During the second year the experimental groups will be assigned to the same room at the same times.

The teachers involved in the experiment must understand the nature and limitations of the study and show no bias toward either group. Two teachers will be selected at random from the available teachers qualified to teach the course. Each teacher will be assigned to one control class and one experimental class.

The content of Honors English will remain identically the same for the two-year period. The same material will be covered in both control and experimental classes. Textbooks and teaching materials will be the same for all classes. The same assignments and tests will be given to all classes.

The basic difference between the control and experimental groups will be in the area of grading. The control classes will be graded on all tests and assignments in the standard fashion for the school—the typical system of letter grades. Final grades will be given at the regular reporting periods. The experimental classes will *not* receive grades for tests and assignments. Each student in the experimental classes will be guaranteed an A grade for the course, regardless of his performance on tests and assignments. No grades will be given at any time during the course, except that each student will be given an A on his final report card. These students will be told, however, that all work in the course must be done in order to receive credit for the course.

At the end of each of the two school years, the students will take a suitable achievement test. If a standardized test cannot be found to measure achievement in a course covering Honors content, then a suitable teacher-made test will have to be employed.

Analysis of data

The mean achievement scores will be computed for the control and experimental groups. Analysis of variance will be used to determine whether or not a significant difference exists at the 10 percent level.

Potential findings and consequences

If the mean scores of the control group are significantly higher than the mean scores of the experimental group, it may be concluded that the traditional method of grading students produces superior achievement in the case of students in Honors English classes in the school(s) in question. In this event, it will be recommended that such classes retain their present grading system. If the mean scores of the experimental groups are significantly higher than those of the control groups, or if the null hypothesis is accepted that no significant difference exists between the groups, it will be recommended that future Honors English classes be nongraded or that they be graded on a pass-fail system.

COMMENTS

This study deals with the effect of the two types of grading practice on achievement in Honors English classes. The researcher wishes to discover whether or not he can modify current practice in favor of what he apparently regards as a better approach, with no loss in academic achievement. If so, he will change practice.

In supporting his choice of study, the author contends that able students avoid Honors classes because of the competition for grades. Interested as they are in the grade-point average that they must present for college admission, they prefer to register for more heterogeneous, unselected classes where they are virtually assured of an A grade. To what extent is this a real phenomenon? Many have attested to its presence (including James B. Conant, former president of Harvard), but few have backed their assertions with hard data.

The researcher advances the hypothesis that the nongraded groups will achieve more than will the graded groups. In other words, he is willing to predict the direction of the difference, if any, between the two groups. However, there is little in the literature that would support the one-tailed (single-direction) approach that such an hypothesis would dictate.

The population selected by the author is typical of populations usually available to the teacher-researcher, who is interested in generalizing the results of his research to future students of the same sort he is teaching currently. Assuming there will be no marked change in the characteristics of such students, he feels comfortable in asserting that whatever will hold true for classes for two years will, in all likelihood, hold true in subsequent years. This would appear to be a reasonable assumption, but one demanding close watch over future conditions.

There is both good and bad in the procedures the investigator would employ. The use of a two-year period for the study illustrates a reasonable solution to a vexing problem in educational research—the "Hawthorne Effect," which involves motivation through special attention. In most experiments of this general type of design, experimental and control classes are conducted simultaneously. In this experiment, however, the difference between treatments is of such a nature that both treatments could not be administered during the same academic year.

On the other hand, the researcher is unreasonably vague about his criterion measure, the achievement test he will administer to the students in the study. Since the outcome of the study hinges in large part upon the validity of the instrument employed, he must take great pains to select an appropriate standardized test, or if none exists (the more likely situation), to describe the instrument he plans to develop for his purpose. Since written composition is a component part of his study, it is highly unlikely that he could find a single test suitable to the study. Also, the author does not define "significantly more" (see "Hypothesis").

The proposed analysis of the data also incorporates

misconceptions. The investigator states analysis of variance as his statistical test. This would lead one to believe that he intends to treat the four groups as separate entities. Yet he speaks only of the experimental and control "programs." With but two treatments, the results for the experimental and control groups might be pooled and the simpler t-test used for analysis.[1] He further assumes that the experimental and control groups are equivalent at the beginning of their respective academic years, but he does not suggest demonstrating this. A pretest on the dependent variable (the outcome) would give more confidence in their initial equivalence.

In his statement of potential findings, the author claims acceptance of the null hypothesis as a favorable outcome for his purposes. This means that the chances thus become nineteen to one (10 percent level) that two years hence all students in Honors English at his high school(s) will be receiving A grades.[2] He also is willing to extend his findings to a pass-fail system even though this was not originally incorporated into his study.

[1] Where the comparison is between only two groups and no interaction analysis is contemplated, there is no particular advantage to be gained using analysis of variance. The t-test is generally easier for the beginning researcher to understand and employ. Normally, analysis of variance is more economically employed with three or more groups.

[2] Some explanation of this statement is probably in order. The author should properly use a "two-tailed" test of significance because there is no prior reason to believe that the difference between the two groups will inevitably be in one direction. Using a two-tailed test, a significant difference in favor of the experimental group could occur by chance only 5 percent of the time. However, the author is also willing to change his practice in favor of the experimental treatment if the null hypothesis is accepted. This could occur by chance 90 percent of the time. Thus the probability for a "favorable" outcome from the point of view of the author is actually 5 plus 90 or 95 percent. Hence the nineteen-to-one odds.

This is an example of a semiexperimental design that could be employed in almost any school situation. It lacks the necessary elements of randomness of selection/treatment and control that would qualify it as a "true" experimental design. Nonetheless, it is a useful approach for the teacher-researcher. This particular design, though, has the weaknesses already mentioned. The outcome of the study virtually can be predicted to be "no significant difference," the typical outcome of most experiments of this type. But it should not be criticized solely on that basis; the author is making a genuine attempt to obtain information on what he regards as a genuine instructional problem. His attempt should be encouraged because, despite surety of outcomes, he is a step up from the status quo, or the intuitive assessment usually made in regard to one method versus another in regards to grading, content, and so on.

Case ten

THE DEVELOPMENT OF
A SINGLE-ITEM BASKETBALL
TEST AS A MEASURE OF
BASKETBALL PLAYING ABILITY
IN ELEVENTH-GRADE BOYS
—A DESCRIPTIVE/PREDICTIVE STUDY

One part of the research process is the development of
new measuring instruments. Once an instrument has been
developed, however, its worth must be demonstrated.
This study presents an elementary example of the
test-validation process in educational research.

The problem

The purpose of this study is to develop a single-item basketball test that will be valid and reliable for predicting basketball ability. A "single-item" test, as here outlined, is one a
player executes in one attempt with a continuous series of
movements yielding a single point score.

Need for the study

Two persistent problems facing any teacher of physical
education are (1) how to equalize teams for good competition, and (2) how to select the best player from a large
group of players. Traditionally, teachers have relied upon
unaided judgment in meeting these two problems. In recent
years test batteries have been developed to aid in making
such decisions, but these test batteries usually consist of a
number of items and take some time to administer. There
is need for an easily administered, short but valid test in
this area.

Hypotheses

There are three research hypotheses for this study.

- there will be a significant, positive correlation between the results of a single-item basketball test and the Knox (validated) Basketball Test.
- there will be a significant positive correlation between the results of the test and the judgments of ability.
- there will be a significant, positive correlation among each of three trials on a single-item basketball test.

Population and sample

The population will consist of all eleventh-grade boys in X High School. A sample of forty boys will be randomly selected from this population. These students will be randomly assigned to two groups, A and B.

Procedures

The testing and validation procedures will be carried out during the first two weeks of the basketball schedule in physical education. Prior to actual testing, each group will be briefly informed of the nature of the study and given a description of the test items in both the Knox Basketball Test and the Single-Item Basketball Test. Immediately before each test is administered, the testers will demonstrate the test procedure. Three class periods will be used for the administration of the tests, in this order:

Period	Group A	Group B
1	Knox Test—Items 1 and 2	Single-Item Test
2	Knox Test—Items 3 and 4	Knox Test—Items 1 and 2
3	Single-Item Test	Knox Test—Items 3 and 4

The Knox Test is a widely used instrument for measuring basketball ability. It consists of four items: (1) dribble shoot, (2) speed dribble, (3) penny cup, and (4) speed pass. Procedures for administering the test are given in the test manual.

The Single-Item Test requires the student to run the complete length of a basketball court and return while performing certain activities. He begins by making a 180-degree turn at one endline, picks up a basketball at the near foul line, dribbles and weaves around four chairs placed between mid-court and the far foul line, passes the ball at a wall target two feet by two feet placed four feet high on the opposite wall, retrieves the ball on the rebound from the wall and return dribbles through the chairs, and shoots the ball into the basket any time after passing the original foul line. An individual's basic score is the total time, measured to the nearest tenth of a second, required to complete the test. To the basic score, two seconds are added for each penalty assessed during the test. A penalty is given for (1) double dribbling, (2) walking with the ball, and (3) failing to bounce the ball within the target area on the far wall. No more than five penalties are to be assessed during any trial. Three trials are given.

Three physical education teachers will judge the basketball ability of the forty boys as they participate in four basketball games. The best player is assigned a mark of 40, the next best 39, and so on.

Analysis of data

Correlational analysis will be applied to the results of the procedures of the study as follows:

- a rank-order coefficient will be calculated using the results of the Single-Item Basketball Test and the pooled rankings of the three teachers.

- a rank-order coefficient will be calculated using raw scores from the Single-Item Basketball Test and the Knox Basketball Test.
- Pearsonian correlations will be calculated for the three trials on the Single-Item Basketball Test.[1]

Potential findings and consequences

As hypothesized, it is anticipated that positive correlations would result from this analysis. To be useful, however, the correlations would have to lie beyond the limits of mere significance. A value of .70 would mark the lower limit of acceptability. If this value is attained, the Single-Item Basketball Test can be assumed to be useful to physical education teachers for measuring basketball ability.

COMMENTS

Test validation studies are not always considered research. However, since the instrument used to measure variables is extremely important, such studies play a legitimate role in educational research. This particular study exemplifies both good and poor procedures.

The researcher makes a reasonably good case for the need for a study of this sort. Physical education teachers do have to match teams, and the closer the matching, the better the competition. When acting as coaches, they must also select what they believe to be the best players. They can be mistaken in this process by overlooking someone with good potential.

---

[1] There are many types of correlation coefficients other than the common Pearsonian or product-moment coefficient. The rank-order coefficient gives an approximation to the product-moment coefficient when the data on at least one of the two variables are in the form of ranks or ordinal data rather than interval data.

As would be expected, the researcher assumes a positive relation between the test he is developing and other indices of basketball ability. He is aware, however, that the correlation coefficient will have to be larger than mere statistical significance in order for the test to be of any functional value.[2]

Although random samples are not strictly necessary in a test validation study, they do tend to ensure a representative sample. The researcher wisely splits his sample into two groups to guard against a possible serial effect of testing. (There is no doubt that performance on one test will affect performance on the other test.)

The procedures employed seem sufficiently straightforward. There may be some doubt about the ability of teachers to rank forty students in order of ability after seeing them in action in only four games. Very likely there would be some unreliability here that will reduce the magnitude of the validity coefficients.

One suggestion for a more direct validation procedure is in order. Since one of the reasons for developing the test is to assemble "equated" teams, the researcher could assemble eight such teams out of the forty boys, using the three different methods of judging basketball ability. He could use the difference in game scores as his criterion and see which of the three approaches produces the lowest total.

The experimenter wisely uses a rank-order coefficient for his initial hypothesis since the pooled judgments of

[2] The magnitude of a correlation coefficient needed to achieve significance (significantly different from zero) depends upon the size of the sample. With a large sample, it may be quite low, say .05. In an applied situation, such a low correlation would have no functional value even though it had statistical significance. A value of .70, for example, accounts for only 49 percent ($.70^2$) of the variance of the criterion. The remainder of the variance is due to other factors.

teachers represent ordinal data.[3] There is no reason, however, why he cannot use the more common product-moment
coefficient for his second hypothesis, since both sets of data
represent scale values.[4]

The researcher sets a minimum acceptable value of
+ .70 for his validity coefficients. In view of the unreliability of some of his measures, this seems a realistic expec-
tation. If the test attains this level, and if it can be demonstrated that it significantly adds anything to teacher
judgment, then the study is probably worth the effort.

[3] Ordinal data are data given only in terms of ranks, when all
we can say is that A is greater than B, B is greater than C, therefore
A is also greater than C. We have no knowledge of the precise difference between A, B, and C. Interval data are based upon measurement scales using a fixed (although arbitrary) zero with nominally
equal units of measurement. A good example would be the typical
Fahrenheit or Centigrade scale for measuring temperature.

[4] Educational researchers typically allow for some latitude
in the interpretation of what constitutes "interval" scales. If error is
to be made, it seems advisable to opt for the type of error arising
from the use of the more refined mathematical techniques permissible
with interval data.

A COMPARISON IN TERMS OF CERTAIN CHARACTERISTICS OF TWO GROUPS OF STUDENTS WHO TRANSFER FROM ONE DISTRICT TO ANOTHER WITHIN A METROPOLITAN SCHOOL SYSTEM UNDER A VOLUNTARY TRANSFER PROGRAM —A DESCRIPTIVE STUDY

This study deals with the effects on certain characteristics of a change in academic/social environment. The reader will recognize both its contemporary importance and its potential application of findings. The proposed study illustrates very directly the mutual involvement of social values, academic programs, and critical current issues.

The problem

Stated directly, the question is: "Do tenth-grade Negro students who voluntarily transfer for three consecutive years from the Central District to receiving schools within another district of the same system differ significantly in regard to attendance, academic grades, aptitude, intelligence scores, and ethnic attitudes when compared to tenth-grade Negro students who transfer for only one or two years?"

The investigator is a teacher within the school system and is particularly interested in a certain portion of the students—those named above—who choose to transfer under an all-district policy, elementary through secondary, that aims at providing students with opportunities to develop more positive relationships with others who have different racial, cultural, and social backgrounds. The investigator states that the program now is several years old and is increasing in scope and number annually. Several hundred high school students now participate, the majority of them Negro.

Need for the study

Although such transfer programs are increasingly common, little is known of the particular factors and their interrelationship that prompt some students but not others to transfer. Within the district in question, more definite information than that available from studies to date is needed for analysis, planning, assessing the changes resulting from transfer, determining the changes and their influence by length of time, and so on. Of particular interest to the investigator are the relationships and changes stated in the following hypotheses.

Hypotheses

- students transferring from out of the Central District and remaining at school for three years in another district will show a significant improvement in their attendance record in comparison to: (a) their ninth-grade, pretransfer attendance records, (b) students transferring for only one or two years
- the same will hold for academic grades
- the same will hold for post-transfer attitudes toward other ethnic groups
- those transferring for three years will show higher aptitude scores than those who transfer for only one or two years
- the same as above for intelligence scores

In each case the statistical hypothesis is stated as the null hypothesis—no significant difference. For all characteristics but attitude, the confidence level is set at .05—95 percent statistical certainty; for attitude it is set at .10—90 percent statistical certainty. (Rejection of the null hypothesis in any one instance would mean acceptance of the correspondent research hypothesis, with the degree of certainty noted.)

Definition of key terms

- *voluntary transfer.* Refers to students who elect to leave their neighborhood school. They may do so if by transferring they improve (help equalize) the racial balance of the school to which they transfer. They must submit proper application forms, etc.
- *improved racial balance.* Balance that is more correspondent to that of the particular ethnic group in the larger community.
- *grades.* The customary letter grades received in courses.
- *attendance.* Means the number of full days or excused days for which a student is credited.
- *attitude.* Refers to the degree of positive or negative affect associated with a person, symbol, idea, etc.
- *aptitude.* Capacity in a given skill or area of knowledge.

Population

The population consists of the total of all such students as described, now and in the immediate future. The sample for the study will consist of 150 students transferring out of the Central District at the beginning of the tenth grade. The sample will be selected from a listing of all such students who indicate they will transfer; then 150 names will be selected randomly (all names will be numbered and 150 chosen by use of a table of random numbers).

Procedures

Data on attendance, academic grades, aptitude, and intelligence will be collected from school records prior to the

transfer of the students. A social distance scale (which de-
termines a measure of tolerance for ethnic groups other than
one's own) also will be administered before transfer. Any
student who has not taken any of the above-named measures
recently will be given that particular measure so that data
and scores will be related in time.

At the end of each succeeding year, information on
attendance and academic grades will be collected. (Such
information up to the tenth grade will be available initially,
of course.) The same social distance scale will be given any
student who leaves before completing three consecutive
years, at the time he leaves.

The social distance scale to be employed will be
given en masse to all students randomly selected during the
period just prior to the start of their tenth year of school.
The scale, a published, tested instrument, will be modified
slightly by eliminating references to ethnic groups that in
the investigator's opinion would be unfamiliar to a majority
of the students involved. Also, three nonexistent groups will
be added to "see if students are prejudiced against a com-
pletely unknown group (generalized prejudice) or if they
would be more tolerant of this group."

Analysis of data

The mean for each characteristic (attendance, etc.) will be
calculated for each group of students: one-, two-, and three-
year transfers. Z-scores (due to the large size of the sample)
will be used to compare the means, with the confidence
levels previously stated employed in accepting or rejecting
the null hypothesis in each instance.

Potential limitations

Those noted by the investigator include:

- no account is taken of physical, mental, and emotional growth except as inferred from scores

- motivation is unaccounted for
- students who drop out of school after reaching age sixteen (the legal leaving age) may be difficult to involve in terminal testing; and some students inevitably will "disappear" without trace, thus diluting the sample
- the repetition of the social distance scale may result in students' providing remembered responses to the first testing
- the interrelationship and elusiveness of attitudes is noted
- teacher and school climate variation are unaccounted for
- no direct account is taken of the chronological age of the students, their sex, their socio-economic backgrounds, their home structures, the number of siblings, and the like

Potential findings and consequences

If the null hypothesis is accepted in any instance, no apparent difference exists as a result of time spent as a transfer student, *according to the design and analysis of the study*. Rejection of a null hypothesis and acceptance of the related research hypothesis speaks for itself. Such findings will call for further testing and will provide guidelines for planning and increasing the program. Rejection will indicate that students can be selected for transfer more accurately by noting those students who prosper best, by suggesting special conditions and preparation needed to help ensure successful transfer, and so on.

COMMENTS

There is no doubt of the potential value of such a study or of its direct consequences on an existing program if significant findings do occur. It is an example of a design aimed at finding out what is—the status of something (here several characteristics)—and what occurs to this "what" as the result of a certain process (here transfer to another school with a different set of social conditions). The design is quite acceptable in many ways, and the investigator has paid close attention to likely obstacles and hazards, although not all have been accounted for or controlled.

First, and obviously, this is a "touchy" area of inquiry. Care, cooperation, and careful planning are necessary in such studies in order to prevent emotional responses and a "guinea pig" feeling on the part of those involved in the testing. School administrators would be wary, although not necessarily obstructive.

The study specifically aims at high school students, but it seems a shame that a group of, say, fifth-graders is not included (assuming the tests could be used with them) for comparison's sake. Would there be a difference, over time, between them and tenth–twelfth grade students in terms of the characteristics named? The power of the study would seem diminished by not taking advantage of such opportunity. Also, since Caucasian students transfer too, why not include a comparative group of them?

The single variables of time and exposure are the crucial variables of the study. But do they alone produce the suggested changes in characteristics? More likely there are many characteristics and conditions mutually operating. Home background, sex, number of siblings, and socio-economic factors doubtless affect any changes that might occur. The investigator, to be fair, notes this in his remarks about possible limitations. But as above, might not some of these factors be accounted for? At least the provision of such information would allow for subcategorization of students and would produce more refined, more precise data. Here, though, a more complex set of multiple correlations and possibly factor analysis would be needed to interpret the data produced.[1] It might be, however, that the investigator could turn for assistance with his design to the district's research director or to competent assistance on a college campus. A really discriminating analysis would be aided by use of a computer, and a program could be developed, or adapted, to provide such analysis.

The possible attrition of the sample may result in a diminution of certain groups to such a small number (say, those who leave after one year) that the statistical device suggested would be inapplicable and another would have to be substituted. If the sample reduced randomly but still was large enough for the proposed treatment, fine and good! Here is a common hazard encountered in a long-range study of most sorts.

This is a good example of a meaningful descriptive study whose purpose is the discovery of relationships and the assumed influence (but not proven as in a tight study where all but the primary independent variable is controlled for) of certain factors on particular characteristics. It has immediate functional and predictive possibilities should the null hypotheses be rejected. But it does not allow one to say with certainty that a change in x (time) caused a change in y (one characteristic or another). Still, it surely is a long step ahead of speculation and hunch, and opens the door to more controlled, more precise investigation.

---

[1] Multiple correlation is the mathematical expression of a relationship among three or more variables. For example, we may wish to find out the magnitude of the relationship between X and the combination of factors Y and Z.

Factor analysis is basically a mathematical process devised to find the "commonality" in a correlation matrix. It is assumed that if two variables are correlated, they must have something "in common." What they have in common is called a "factor." It is the purpose of factor analysis to extract these factors in order to help explain what accounts for the observed relationship among variables.

BASIC OBJECTIVES EMPLOYED IN TEACHING HISTORY IN GERMAN SCHOOLS SINCE 1900 —AN HISTORICAL INQUIRY

The problem

The author, a secondary school teacher with an undergraduate major in European history, is interested in determining the basic objectives of the history taught in German public schools since about 1900. He is also interested in attempting to determine the influence of the prevailing national political structures and ideologies in shaping these objectives. The author notes that he spent a number of years teaching in the public school system of Germany before moving to America.

Need for the study

"Certainly every teacher who takes seriously the verbal reconstruction of past events . . . has experienced the mental quandary about basic aims in the instruction of history . . . . And while on the primary and secondary levels the teacher does not engage in the direct communication of a philosophy of history to the pupils, he will himself never allow the search for basic objectives and approaches to cease."

The point is also made that the researcher has found no published systematic attempt to trace basic aims in the instruction of history in German schools during the period he suggests.

Hypothesis

That the basic objectives employed in teaching history in German schools since about 1900 were determined mainly by the prevailing political structure and ideology of the particular time.

Population

The population and sample in this case consist of documents, records, publications of one sort or another, and interviews. These are discussed later.

Procedures

The investigator would devote some attention to the period 1800–1900 in order to provide a setting against for his study (1900–present). Then, turning his attention to the period in question, he would search out and utilize as sources the following materials:

- **Primary**
  government constitutions
  directives (ministry and district) to teachers
  curricula on history
  texts
  lesson outlines and syllabi
  films, recordings, interviews with teachers

- **Secondary**
  books, documents, journals, etc. that discuss, interpret, or evaluate the above materials, including novels, conference discussions, reports, and the like

The materials used would derive from or relate to five main periods of German political structure since 1900: (1) the constitutional monarchy, (2) the Weimar Republic, (3) the Nazi period, (4) the occupation government, (5) the Federal Republic.

The treatment of the data would be analytic and comparative, identifying first the prevailing political and ideological structure of the country and then identifying the major objectives assumed to have influenced the teaching of history. Comparison would be developed among the periods stated.

The investigator notes certain major difficulties: access to materials (including translations), the effect of individual teachers and school subunits, the necessity to limit his survey of materials but to include both important and representative sources, the choice of the prevailing ideology, the assumption that there were nationally employed objectives, and so on. But he also points out his command of German, his familiarity with the present German school system, some acquaintance with certain sources and their location, and possible sponsorship of the project.

Potential findings and consequences

These are stated in "Need for the study." Otherwise, a possible addition to educational-historical knowledge is suggested.

COMMENTS

Certainly the scope of the study is such that few graduate students would be bold enough or able enough to undertake it. More than likely, a group of mature scholars or the rare individual with cross-disciplinary talents in history, political science, and social philosophy would undertake such an enterprise. Yet both the history of education and comparative education provide examples of single ventures toward such knowledge.

The investigator's statement that no such studies exist would have to be challenged; a few hours in a college library with holdings in the history of education and in comparative education would unearth publications related to his intended research, although additional research efforts would hardly be unacceptable. Yet given these conditions, the study proposed exemplifies the historical-analytic approach to educational investigation and illustrates many of the elements and difficulties of such an approach.[1]

There is little doubt that prevalent political structures and ideologies affect the teaching of social science, especially of history. George Orwell's *1984* provides a chill reminder. So do the Third Reich and various present governments. In the United States, the call for a reexamination of the history and contributions of the Negro hits closer to home. From the time of Plato, emphasis has been placed on the presentation of history, or its reconstruction, to harmonize with current political and social aims or to justify and explain them. That the investigator's hypothesis is apt to be confirmed is not surprising. The degree and methods employed during different political and ideological regimes are of primary concern here.

First, the matter of terms. A change in the legal or enforced form of government occurs at a time that can be dated, but when does change occur (in this instance in the teaching of history) in institutions or programs within the body politic? Does the author intend to trace, by sample here and there, such change from a particular date; or from,

---

[1] More typical investigations, ones that teachers or graduate students in education might deal with, include the development of curricula or policies or programs in a certain district or region; the history of financing and related difficulties in a school system; the matter of censorship in one form or another; the involvement of the public in certain school activities or programs; and many more. These are usually directed at understanding the present condition of something or are aimed at helping predict likely outcomes in light of past events or factors. This type of study is not so common as it should be, for ordinarily it deals with matters of no little concern. That it takes special talent and analytic ability is evident, and that it takes time is equally apparent.

say, the midpoint of the periods he selects? What does he mean by period?

What does he mean by "history classes"? All such classes so called? Courses incorporating history into their curriculum? What? Since selection will have to be made from this population, definition of the population is demanded. Also key to his proposed study is his definition of "objectives." Does he mean the explicit, stated objectives or the inferred objectives (from examination of such documents as curriculum guides), or both? The one is easier to identify than the other.

In suggesting sources of materials, he frames two common categories: primary (direct) and secondary (derivative) materials. This is not uncommon. But the weight to be given to each and how one would check against the other or supplement the other need to be developed. Such matters as authenticity of material, objectivity of source, accuracy of translation or record, and so on come into play.[2]

Interviews provide a potentially fruitful source, both for obtaining direct information and impressions and for checking data otherwise obtained. But, as noted elsewhere in this casebook, interviews demand skill, practice, and considerable selectivity. Would the investigator be capable of this or would he need assistance?

The skills involved in excerpting vital information from available sources are considerable. The investigator must have his design (as in other research designs) well in hand to enable him to identify and use information that is relevant and to overlook that which is not.

[2] See bibliography suggestions at the end of this casebook for selections that deal with the historical approach, with matters of internal and external criticism, etc. Most of the general titles on educational research contain either such information or some leads to specific, more exhaustive references.

His powers of critical analysis and of synthesis must be well above average, as must his ability to record his results in an objective and organized narrative. Historical fact (as best can be determined) is one thing; its presentation another. Skill in organizing and writing are of equal importance with skill in identifying, selecting, assembling, and synthesizing data.

The factors of time and necessary resources to conduct such a study as here proposed make this more of a hypothetical exercise than a likelihood, at least in the present case.

This is an example of an educational inquiry that lends itself to the historical-comparative approach. Paramount are the skill and analytic ability of the investigator, since he is responsible for all elements of the design and the interpretation of data. (No "canned" formulas are to be followed, no .01 certainty, etc. However, there exists a body of experience, methodology, and precept to serve as a guide). Unquestionable, however, is the value of the proposed study and ones like it; the interaction of curriculum and social-political elements is and always has been the name of the educational game, whether microscopic (local bond levies and their ups and downs) or macroscopic (the influence of the social and cultural heritage and expectations on the national curriculum of the schools).

THE TRANSFER EFFECT OF A DIRECT TEACHING METHOD IN READING AT THE PRIMARY LEVEL —A QUASI-EXPERIMENTAL STUDY

This chapter presents a study about transfer, one of the basic problems in learning research. In general, transfer occurs when material or skills learned in one situation can be used effectively in a different but somewhat similar situation. The skill involved in this study is a reading skill.

The problem

It is the purpose of this study to investigate the possibility of potential inhibitory effects associated with the transfer to double-column reading material when children are taught to read from single-column basal readers.

Need for the study

The basal readers used at the primary level almost universally consist of material presented in single-column format. However, much of the supplementary reading material in the content areas is presented in double-column format. Teachers have frequently observed that students have difficulty transferring the skills acquired in their basal readers to double-column materials without additional supplementary instruction on "how to read" double-column material. Would the need for such supplementary instruction be eliminated by incorporating a direct method of learning to read double-column material into the basal reading program?

Hypothesis

The hypothesis for this study is that second-grade children learning reading under a modified basal reading program that incorporates one day of instruction per week on double-column material will make fewer mistakes when reading new, double-column material than will similar children whose basal reading program consists only of single-column material. The implied but not stated (statistical) null hypothesis is that groups will not differ significantly in terms of the dependent variable (reading errors of a certain kind, as explained later).

Population and sample

The population for this study will consist of all second-grade students at X Elementary School. A stratified, random sample of sixty students will be selected for the study. Stratification (selection of ability levels) will be based on the scores of a standardized reading test administered the previous spring at the end of the first grade.

Procedures

The sixty students selected for the sample will be assigned at random to two classes. Reading instruction in one class will be by the usual basal reader using single-column material. The second class will use the same instructional material for four days of the week. On the fifth day, however, direct instruction on the reading of double-column material will be presented. Such material will be equated with the single-column material used by the other class on the variables of readability, legibility, and visibility.

The experimental treatments will continue for a ten-week period. At the end of that time each child in both groups will be asked to read aloud a page of double-column material that he has not previously seen. His performance will be recorded by a tape recorder.

Analysis of data

The performances recorded on the tapes will be analyzed by counting the number of errors that occur. Only one type of error is relevant to this study: the error that occurs when the student continues to read on a given line across the center margin of the page to the corresponding line on the right-hand side of the page. The number of such errors for each student will be recorded. The Mann-Whitney U Test[1] will be used to determine if a significant difference exists between the two groups on the number of such errors committed. A one-tailed test will be used, and significance will be set at the .05 level.

Potential findings and implications

If the research hypothesis is supported by the evidence from this study, and a difference is found in favor of the experimental treatment, second-grade teachers at X Elementary School will incorporate direct training on double-column material into their basal reading program. If the null hypothesis is accepted, no change will be made in the basal reading program, and students will continue to be taught using single-column materials exclusively.

COMMENTS

The title of this study is somewhat misleading. It might appear from the title that only the transfer effects of the one treatment are under study. Actually, transfer effects from two different types of treatment are under consideration. Moreover, the effects of the experimental treatment could scarcely be considered transfer effects since this treatment is

[1] The Mann-Whitney U Test is an example of the type of test of significance statisticians call "nonparametric" tests. By this they mean that the data collected from a sample are not used to estimate any population parameters, and hence, assumptions about the population need not act as restrictions upon the use of such tests. Since the most common of these assumptions is that the population is normally distributed, nonparametric tests are sometimes called "distribution-free" techniques. The particular test suggested here, the

actually direct instruction on the dependent variable for the study. It is only the control treatment that might be said to exhibit transfer effects, since it uses materials somewhat different from those employed for assessing the dependent variable.

The author presents no evidence other than his own opinion that difficulties in transferring from single-column materials to double-column materials do, in fact, occur in second-grade children. Is this a common phenomenon posing a difficult instructional problem for the teachers?

The research hypothesis seems to be reasonably well stated. Notice that later the author proposes to test the corresponding null hypothesis using a one-tailed test. Presumably this reflects his implicit recognition that direct instruction on the dependent variable *ought* to produce an experimental effect greater than the transfer effect of indirect instruction.

The author fails to state the size of the population. Presumably there are more than two second-grade classrooms in the school. He seems reasonably confident that each of his sample of sixty students could be assigned at random to one of two classrooms. In practice, this is frequently difficult to do. Although he stratified his population on reading achievement, he did not stratify them on sex. Sex has typically been demonstrated to be an important factor in reading studies.

Certain questions can be raised regarding the experimental procedures. First of all, is ten weeks a sufficient length of time to demonstrate any differential effect? During this period, the experimental group would receive only ten

---

Mann-Whitney U Test, requires that the data be transformed into ranks. The ranks for each treatment are summed. A statistic called *U* is calculated using these sums and the *N*'s for the two groups. The statistic *U* is converted to a *z* score, and the normal table is used to establish the probability level of the outcome.

exposures to the experimental treatment. Each exposure would probably last something less than an hour. Reading achievement is a variable that changes only slowly, particularly at the initial stages of instruction. Next, the investigator fails to mention whether one or two teachers are involved in the study. Since this is a methods study, regardless of what it is called by the author, the teacher variable can be a crucial one. In most studies of this type using two teachers, the contribution to error variance of the *teacher* variable may be sufficiently great to vitiate the entire design.

Additional questions may be raised concerning the test used to measure the dependent variable and the analysis of the results from this test. First, the author does not indicate whether the same page of reading material will be used for all sixty students. Since we know that even at the second-grade level reading ability may vary widely (as well as content difficulty page by page), would the same reading material be appropriate as a test for all students? What about the nonreader? How would he be scored? Next, there is no indication of how many errors might be expected from a single page of test material. If the number of such errors is relatively small, there would be many tied ranks on the Mann-Whitney U Test, which would result in a lowered sensitivity of this test. One might also question whether the more powerful parametric techniques might not be employed instead of the nonparametric technique proposed. In practice, error scores are frequently taken to represent interval data, and if the assumptions for the parametric techniques were reasonably well satisfied, their use could be defended in a study of this type.

Although this study has many deficiencies, the investigator does isolate a single, definable problem. He fails, however, to establish the importance of this problem, and the procedures he proposes may not be such that he could give a definitive answer at the conclusion of his study.

A COMPARISON OF THE EVALUATION OF TEACHER PERFORMANCE BY PRINCIPALS AND TEACHERS —A DESCRIPTIVE STUDY

The definition and evaluation of what constitutes good teaching is a controversial and sensitive issue in education. The issue to be investigated in the study proposed in this chapter is how well teachers and administration can agree on what they see when they observe teaching performance.

The problem

It is the purpose of this study to investigate the degree of relationship between evaluations of teacher performance made by principals and evaluations of the same performance made by fellow teachers.

Need for the study

When teacher performance is evaluated for whatever reasons, such evaluations are normally made by administrative or supervisory personnel. This procedure has certain disadvantages. First, teachers tend to distrust such evaluations because they feel that the evaluator is not himself a teacher and thus is too remote from the classroom to make valid judgments. Next, the professional "distance" between teacher and supervisor or administrator increases as a concomitant of the process. It is apparent, however, that such evaluations must be conducted, especially if the movement toward merit pay for excellence in teaching becomes more pronounced. The basic question is, "Can teachers do as good a job of evaluating the performance of their peers as administrators now do?"

Population and sample

The population for this study will consist of all teachers in X School District. From this population ten teachers will be chosen as a sample. It is the teaching performance of these ten individuals that will be evaluated.

Procedures

An evaluation "team" consisting of three persons will be set up for each building in the district. This team will consist of the principal of the school, one teacher from that school, and one teacher from another school. This team will visit the classroom of the teacher selected for the evaluation and observe his performance for a period of one hour. At the end of the hour, each member of the team will independently fill out a standard evaluation rating sheet on the performance of the teacher, as he observed it. This rating sheet consists of a number of traits to be evaluated on a scale from one to five. The rating sheets will be turned in to the investigator.

Analysis of data

The data will consist of thirty evaluations, three from each of ten schools (ten teachers). These data will be treated by chi-square analysis to see if the distribution of ratings to the five possible response categories for each trait in the evaluation rating sheet is different for principals and teachers. If the chi-square analysis shows that the ratings are not significantly different from each other, then a contingency coefficient[1] will be calculated as an estimate of the relation

[1] The contingency coefficient is another type of correlation coefficient. It is calculated using an obtained value of chi-square. It does not have the same range of values as the more common product-moment coefficient and cannot be interpreted in exactly the same way. It does, however, serve as a useful index of relationship where the original data are reported as frequencies within classification categories.

between ratings given by principals and those given by teachers.

Potential findings and consequences

Many administrative decisions are made on the basis of teacher evaluations. In addition to the matter of merit pay already discussed, there are decisions on tenure, dismissal, or possibly hiring. If it can be demonstrated that fellow teachers evaluate performance in much the same way as principals, then principals can use teams of teachers to help in making such decisions.

COMMENTS

From a professional point of view it can certainly be argued that teachers ought to play a larger role in the evaluation of their peers. It may be somewhat questionable, however, to bolster this assertion by using evidence demonstrating that teachers think the same way as principals about the act of teaching. The fact that two sets of judgments agree does not mean that either one is right. In measurement terms, reliability is not the same as validity.

Certain points are not made sufficiently clear by the researcher. First, how are the ten teachers to be selected for the study? Are they to be selected in some systematic fashion, or will they be volunteers? If they are volunteers, will this not introduce an unknown bias into the study? May it not also reduce the potential variability in teaching performance because volunteers might typically be better-than-average teachers? Would the teachers represent different grades and subjects? If so, what effects would this have? If variability of performance is reduced, it would be more difficult to demonstrate the relationship the researcher desires to establish. Next, we could ask the same question about method of selection for the two teachers who are to be members of the evaluation team. Would the method of selecting these two individuals influence the outcome of the study?

We might also question the adequacy of the data. We have, after all, thirty evaluation forms spread out over thirty evaluators and ten "evaluatees." No evaluator evaluates more than one teacher. Thus there would be no way of estimating his reliability as an evaluator. Moreover, with data spread so thinly, any value of the contingency coefficient one might calculate could give misleading results. If any expected cell frequencies are smaller than five, which could certainly be the case with such data, the resulting coefficient could be quite erroneous.

In general, this is a well-intentioned study that does not quite come off. The justification for peer evaluations of teacher performance might better be made on logical grounds than on the basis of studies such as this one.

A RETROSPECTIVE ANALYSIS OF SUCCESS OR FAILURE OF SPECIAL SCHOOL DISTRICT LEVIES IN THE COMMUNITIES OF COUNTY X —AN HISTORICAL INQUIRY

This study is proposed by a school administrator who, having experienced the consequences of an unsuccessful special levy, is interested in determining if examination of past special levies in his county can provide some set of characteristic conditions or activities that seem to typify successful and unsuccessful efforts.

The problem

It is the investigator's purpose to determine whether or not issues and circumstances that seemed to exist in particular communities that successfully promoted and passed special school levies differ systematically in any way from the circumstances and issues that were current in communities failing to pass such levies. For the focus of his study he has chosen the communities included in the county in which he now is employed. These communities number seven (separate school districts). The period of time with which he is concerned extends forward from the close of World War II—approximately twenty-five years. Totally, the number of such special levies is twenty-three. All districts (communities) had at least two such special levies.

Need for the study

The effects of passage or failure of a special school levy are numerous. Parents, teachers, administrators, and students are directly involved in these consequences. Knowledge about the factors conducive to success or failure would prove instructive.

Hypothesis

The hypothesis for this study is that there exists a set of conditions, absolutely or as a matter of degree, that characterize a successful levy, as well as a set of conditions or issues that characterize an unsuccessful levy; and that these conditions are both general (pervasive throughout districts or communities) and particular (related to a particular district or to success or failure of a special levy). Implied, of course, is that categorization can be made.

Definition of key terms

- *special levy.* One that appears on the ballot for particular purposes (for earmarked expenditures).
- *success and failure.* Means that voters in sufficient numbers endorse or do not endorse (pass) the levy as stated on the ballot.

Population

This is stated as the total number of special levies, as previously defined, that occurred in the county in question during the period 1945–1969: twenty-three levies in all. No sample is involved except insofar as the communities in which the levies were voted on and the conditions existing at the time of voting might be reflected elsewhere.

Procedures

The investigator intends to gather data concerning the communities in question from sources such as county records (assessor, treasurer), state reports on the economic and social features of the several school districts, morgue files of local newspapers, interviews with selected persons in the community who were present and eligible to vote at the

time of the levies, students who were in school at the time
of the levies, and—if possible—persons who were active
either in promoting or resisting the levy. First, he would describe the communities (districts) in terms of size, average
income, population density and mobility, predominant type
of occupation(s), percentage of church membership, and
registration by political party. Next, he would describe the
communities by number of students (at the time of each
levy) in K–12, number and percentage of seniors entering
college upon graduation, median level of schooling of adults
registered to vote in the levies, average per-pupil expenditure of the districts for K–12 education, and percentage of
teacher turnover during the year prior to each levy.

From these data, obtained through the approaches
earlier stated, the investigator would categorize each community; first, according to the variables dealing with social
and economic factors; next, according to the educational
variables. In addition, he would develop an "intensity scale"
for each community for each levy according to the apparent
effort put into passing or defeating the levy and the relative
amount of publicity accompanying each levy. His sources
for this information would consist of newspaper lineage devoted to the levy, information obtained from radio records
and logs (such as might be available), and records of such
organizations as the local PTA's.

Treatment of data

Upon accumulating the types of data mentioned, the investigator would profile each levy in terms of the economic,
social, educational, communications, etc., variables and their
intensity (or ratios or totals depending on type of data).
He then would look comparatively at the profiles of districts
of similar size to determine if certain characteristics appeared commonly for successful or unsuccessful levies. Next
he would compare all districts against the same purpose to

determine if certain characteristics appeared in successful or unsuccessful levies, notwithstanding size. If so, he would categorize the similarities—by district size or in whatever dimension they appeared.

Having done this, he would identify the stated purpose of the individual levies (instructional supplies, salaries, buildings, etc.) and then check them against success or failure according to type of purpose. To do so, he would of course have to select categories of purposes—e.g., curriculum, salary, capital projects, multiple, etc. Finally, he would compare success and failure, purpose of levy, and all other factors both singly and in cluster: economic, social, educational, communicative, and so on. His final presentation of data would be a listing of variables, if any, that seemed to signify success or failure, with an attempt at explaining their apparent effect.

Potential findings and implications

His hypothesis would be confirmed or denied by his collection, treatment, and presentation of data. If certain issues and characteristics appeared related to success or failure, the profiles developed might be of use as "weathervanes" in choosing the conditions and times for future special levies.

COMMENTS

A person who called this study modest would describe Macbeth as unmotivated. One can agree that the purpose as stated is laudable, that the question posed is intriguing, and that the approach described is retrospective analysis— more historical/descriptive than anything else. An analysis of variables might indeed show some that seemed to be associated with success or with failure of a levy according to the type of levy, the size of the community, the generality of the variable, and so on. But to imply cause and effect would be dangerous indeed.

First of all, the number of districts is large contrasted with the number of levies that constitutes the population of the study. Some districts may have had but two levies; others, half a dozen. Even if there were several times the number of levies, coincidence and *not* cause and effect is all that could be claimed. (In fairness, it should be noted that the investigator does not claim to suggest cause and effect, although the implication is there.) If several levies occurred in a single district and not all were of the same outcome, a comparative analysis within that district might well be more productive than a cross-comparative analysis.

Then there is the matter of data collection. What is proposed would occupy a team of researchers for some time. Examination of records, interviews, and all the approaches named suggest an enormous expenditure of time and effort unless a well-developed and representative sampling technique were employed. Also, in collecting data the investigator would have to develop and pretest his procedures for recording information. Each variable would have to have a consistent information and recording approach associated with it. The investigator also would need a workable system of storing and retrieving the data he intends to produce in such amounts.

His selection of variables to be examined is not explained. No doubt he has selected many potentially important ones. But what has he excluded? For such economic, social, communication or other variable, one can suggest an alternative choice (except for perhaps a few obvious "musts"). What rationale for selecting these particular variables is operative? Does the literature suggest that these variables are important? Crucial? Likely to be controlling? Exclusive? Or are they ones that seemed to the investigator to be worthy candidates for inclusion and investigation? There is a difference.

Are there certain variables that might be pervasive but are likely to be seen as localized? For example, could there be the effect of a county-wide economic factor that is most visible in a certain place or for which accurate records are kept in one place but not in another—e.g., welfare or unemployment. Could there be the influence of an outside authority or policy that is not recognized at all but that has unequal effect among communities or districts—e.g., media subscriptions. If not randomly distributed, such variables could have significant effects and the investigator might possibly never become aware of this. (Such hazard is a matter of degree and can be minimized by thorough analysis and reflection before attempting an investigation and by thorough familiarity—either personal or borrowed—with the target area, population, and environment.)

The selection of persons to be interviewed is not discussed. This source of data might be very valuable or virtually worthless. How one voted twenty-five years ago can be adjusted by how one now is inclined to vote or how one now perceives the "correct" answer. Likewise, memories become selective. Then random sampling might be applied to the strata. Even so, judgment would have to temper the use of data obtained—as with other subjective sources.

The treatment, or manipulation, of data apparently is to be by hand. Considering the number of variables involved and the potentially huge number of single and cluster comparisons, the investigator should key punch his data, probably by district and perhaps using several key punch cards for each district. Then machine sorting could pick out the similarities and the differences he seeks.

There are many more objections that could be raised. The availability of data? The relative objectivity of similar types of data—e.g., committee records, news accounts? Such devices as "intensity scales" are tricky to construct and use, although they are employed systematically against all appropriate data. The definition of "intensity" is arbitrary, and one must be certain, or as certain as possible, that the orders of magnitude assigned the scales are not so out of proportion as to override other data for which a less dramatic or more objective measure is employed.

Yet the investigator still might have something going for him—given just enough adjustments to eliminate factors that make the study unbearably difficult or not worth attempting. Knowledge, even incomplete, about conditions existing during past special levies is valuable if it is used with necessary reservations. It could be helpful in directing attention to what seem to be critical factors or issues. It could help with current polling or interviewing by directing questioning to certain apparent problems. It could point out some apparent comparative, differential, or universal factors. It could serve as the prelude to more exact approaches to achieve the same purposes. But he who would prophesy (or make unequivocal statements of fact) from findings based on the approach here described had better own a fast car.

PART TWO:
SELF-STUDY EXERCISES

This section of the casebook provides twelve self-study exercises exclusive of critical commentary. These exercises follow the format used earlier in presenting cases 1–15 and are representative of the types of studies included in the fifteen cases.

In analyzing and criticizing, the reader may follow the format used earlier, or he may examine the exercises by applying a format of his own or one provided by a course instructor. Whatever the approach, the exercises offer an opportunity to apply critical faculties and techniques to a set of exercises which, like the preceding cases, were developed by practitioners as potential studies to be conducted in a particular educational setting. And like the earlier cases, these exercises are some distance from being ready to attempt. Some, in fact, would best be consigned to oblivion, while others would provide a worthy expenditure of effort given certain improvements. Which are which? And why?

DIFFERENCES IN ECONOMIC LITERACY AMONG SPECIFIED GROUPS OF GRADUATING SENIORS IN TWO HIGH SCHOOLS IN THE SAME COMMUNITY

This is an economic world, according to both the investigator of this proposed study and a rather notable listing of supportive writers in one or another areas. Do high school graduates have any understanding of basic economic terms and concepts? Do they gain this through a specific course in economics? Through a related course? Without any specific course? These are questions this study approaches.

The problem

To determine differences in economic literacy among three specified groups of graduating high school seniors: (1) those having had a course in economics, (2) those having had related courses such as business, bookkeeping, etc., and (3) those having had neither (1) nor (2).

Need for the study

It is increasingly necessary for citizens to comprehend economic terms and meanings, and there is limited information available about the effectiveness of specific high school courses to produce such knowledge or familiarity.

Hypothesis

Students in subgroup A will exhibit greater economic literacy than will students in subgroups B or C.

Definition of key terms

- *economics.* Involves the study of materials and procedures related to the creation of goods and services, the management of the process of production, the distribution of goods, and the extent and nature of consumption of goods and services.

- *economic concepts.* Include ideas used to explain specific economic aspects.
- *norms.* Are standard types or patterns.
- *standardized test.* One composed of empirically selected materials, with directions for use, scoring and evaluation, and comparison.
- *subgroup A* Includes students with a course in economics but not a course in related fields.
- *subgroup B.* Includes students with no course in economics but with one in a related field.
- *subgroup C.* Includes students without a course in either economics or a related field.

Population and sample

The population includes graduating seniors from two rather large high schools over a three-year period. The sample will consist of about six hundred students drawn from the senior classes of the two schools.

Special materials

A standardized test of economic understanding that emphasizes terminology and concepts, prepared by the Joint Council on Economic Education.

Procedures

First, permission and cooperation will be sought from administrators and teachers who are to be involved. Next, the test of economic understanding will be given to approximately three hundred seniors in each school; this will include the students' knowledge prior to graduation.

Then the test results will be compared with data furnished by the Joint Council on Economic Education—

designers of the standardized test. Data will be obtained on students' IQ, grade-point average, courses taken in economics, and courses taken in related areas. Data will be categorized into specific listings.

Analysis of data

Analysis of variance, with the null hypothesis to be tested at the .05 level of confidence.

Potential findings and consequences

The investigator notes several potential weaknesses in the study, then states that in addition to obvious potential findings (e.g., students with economics will do better):

- the null hypothesis, if accepted, would indicate that for the purposes in mind a course in economics or related subjects makes little difference
- IQ, grade-point average, or such factors may be of more (assumed) consequence than direct course work in terms of the learning and retention of economic concepts and definitions

THE RELATIONSHIP BETWEEN ROCK 'N' ROLL MUSIC AND AUDITORY FATIGUE

Virtually all adults and neighbors of teen-agers probably would agree, protectively, that loud music—e.g., rock 'n' roll—produces harmful physical effects if one listens to it too much and too long. This study sets up a situation in which the question is attacked under certain conditions.

The problem

Does exposure to rock 'n' roll music affect auditory acuity?

Need for the study

Ask any parent or neighbor of a teen-ager! More seriously, this is a question receiving increasing attention lately, considering the amplification of sound; the amount of exposure students (and others) have to loud, insistent music; and the speculation that harmful physical effects may result.

Hypotheses

The first hypothesis is that there will be no difference in auditory threshold levels measured prior to and after exposure to a stated amount of rock 'n' roll music. The second is that there will be no difference in auditory threshold levels measured just before and two hours after such exposure.

Definition of key terms

- *acoustic trauma.* The sudden loss of hearing caused by exposure to loud sounds.

- *acuity.* Refers to sensitivity of the auditory apparatus; sharpness of hearing.
- *auditory threshold.* That point in the range of increasing intensities of the auditory stimulus at which sensation first appears; the lowest intensity adequate to produce an awareness of stimulation.
- *decibel.* The ratio between the intensities of two tones differing so slightly that, under laboratory conditions, the hearer is barely able to detect a difference in loudness.
- *normal hearing perception.* Involves no clinical or historical evidence of hearing disability.
- *sound pressure level.* Refers to the ratio between sound pressure and a standard reference pressure.
- *temporary threshold shift.* The temporary loss of auditory acuity due to brief exposure to intense noise.

Population and sample

The population is college students with normal hearing perception, who take no drugs or alcohol during the experiment, and who are enrolled in a certain required (large) general education course. The sample is forty-eight such students, twenty-four men and twenty-four women, who meet the previous criteria and who volunteer for the experiment.

Special conditions

The instruments used are to be located in a sound-treated room of the college for the initial testing and in another special room for the experiment. Audiometers will be used to measure hearing levels during the experiment.

Procedures

After initial testing, students are to be told they have been chosen to participate in an experiment involving their hearing. Volunteers (after being assured that no permanent damage to hearing will occur) then will be subjected to a reasonably loud signal, based on individual, pretested capacity. Attenuation will follow in 5- or 10-decibel steps until no auditory response is indicated by the individual. Three consistent response levels will be obtained at each frequency involved to establish a threshold for each frequency. This constitutes the norming phase of the experiment, individual by individual.

Following this, subjects are to assemble at a specified time to listen to "live" rock 'n' roll music supplied by a band. The subjects can listen or dance, either or both, during the two-hour period. At the end of two hours, testing will occur, following the previously described sequences. Then volunteers will go to a lounge to wait two hours for the next testing.

Analysis of data

The primary treatment involves comparison of the three major test scores: (1) pretest, (2) immediately after hearing the music, and (3) two hours later. Secondary analysis involves comparison of variability of thresholds at certain levels—e.g., 500 cycles per second, 2000 cycles per second. Analysis of variance is the statistical procedure to be used. (The investigator then notes certain limitations to the proposed study which are not included here.)

Potential findings and implications

These seem to speak for themselves, although it is doubted that science would triumph over art, even if severe hearing disability is noted.

A STUDY OF CURRENT ATTITUDES OF MALE TEACHERS TOWARD ELEMENTARY SCHOOL INSTRUCTION

Although some progress has been made in the past few years, we still have an insufficient number of men teaching in the elementary schools. What is the reason for this? Perhaps a major factor is the attitudes male teachers hold toward elementary school teaching.

The problem

The purpose of this study is to identify the major factors underlying either positive or negative attitudes of male teachers toward teaching at the elementary school level.

Need for the study

More male teachers are needed in the elementary schools. If men are reluctant to teach at this level because of certain prevailing attitudes held by them or by others, identifying such attitudes will help in dealing with them. Such information would be valuable both to recruiters from the school districts and to college personnel charged with the preparation of teachers.

Hypotheses

There are four research hypotheses for this study:

- there will be a significant difference between the attitudes of prospective male teachers and in-service male teachers at the secondary level as to why they did not choose elementary teaching
- there will be a significant difference between the attitudes of prospective male teachers and in-

service male teachers at the elementary school level as to why they did choose elementary school teaching

- there will be a significant difference between prospective secondary and prospective elementary school male teachers regarding their attitudes toward elementary school teaching
- there will be a significant difference between in-service secondary and in-service elementary school male teachers regarding their attitudes toward elementary school teaching

Population and sample

There are four populations to be used for this study:

- all male secondary school teachers in district X
- all male elementary school teachers in the same district
- all prospective male secondary school teachers in their senior year enrolled at College X
- all prospective male elementary school teachers in their senior year enrolled at the same college

The sample will be a random sample of fifteen persons from each of the four populations.

Procedures

Each of the sixty individuals selected for the sample will receive two questionnaires and have a personal interview by the researcher. The first questionnaire will be open-ended and unstructured. It will simply ask the respondent to give his personal reasons why a man either prefers or does not prefer to teach at the elementary school level. These responses will then be used to develop a set of questions that will be incorporated into a structured questionnaire to be sent to the same individuals. Finally, each member of the sample will be interviewed by the researcher as a check upon the reliability of the answers given previously.

Analysis of data

The analysis will be made on the data received from the second questionnaire. Chi-square will be used to determine whether significant differences in attitude exist among the four groups, based upon the manner in which their responses to the items of the questionnaire are distributed. The .05 level will be used to determine significance.

Potential findings and consequences

This study is designed to discover potential differences in attitude among four groups of people, two groups of experienced male teachers and two groups of prospective male teachers. Should no differences be found, all groups could be said to exhibit the same attitudes. Should differences be found in the experienced-inexperienced dichotomy, teaching experience may be said to influence attitude. Should differences be found in the elementary-secondary dichotomy, other personal characteristics associated with this choice probably determine attitudes toward elementary school teaching.

THE APPLICATION OF A
PARTICULAR READING PROGRAM
IN JUNIOR HIGH SCHOOL
REMEDIAL READING CLASSES

Nothing is more vital to success in school than reading ability. But what about the student who does not like to read, or who is retarded in this vital skill? Can methods and contents be selected that will encourage him to develop a taste for reading and at the same time reduce his disability? The study proposed below approaches this question.

The problem

Will a program similar to that of *Hooked on Books*,[1] utilizing such materials alone and with little direct teaching, occasion as much improvement in reading among junior high school remedial readers as will a more traditional remedial program in reading? The measurement device to be used is a standardized test.

Need for the study

The necessity to improve reading skills speaks for itself. With remedial readers the need is all the more acute. There is considerable difference of opinion about the most productive method of improving the reading abilities of such students. Does a sequential program emphasizing the application of particular skills offer the best approach? Does the free reading of interesting materials, especially pocket books,

---

[1] Daniel N. Fader and Elton B. McNeil. *Hooked on Books: Program and Proof*. New York: Berkeley Publishing Corporation, 1968.

offer more promise with such students? More information is needed; hence this study. The literature suggests that the use of materials of high interest is particularly productive.

Hypothesis

The use of paperbacks, magazines, newspapers, and journal articles—with little direct teaching involved—will bring equal or greater gains to students than will a more traditional, sequential approach. The null hypothesis is that there will be no significant difference in reading achievement gain between two groups, one using the "free" approach, the other the structured approach, as measured by mean scores of the two groups at the end of the experiment.

Assumptions underlying the hypothesis are:

- remedial reading students at the junior high level usually are failures in reading via conventional methods of teaching, and as a result are discouraged and unmotivated
- most such students know more than they are able to demonstrate in class work or on tests. Interesting materials will unlock their potentials better than will ordinary materials/approaches
- interest is the key to reading improvement for such students; it may compensate plus for lack of skills
- such students need reading practice more than they do instruction in reading

Population

The experimenter plans to conduct the study in overseas (European) junior high schools maintained for children of U.S. personnel. All students referred by English or reading teachers constitute the population. The investigator is not clear about this, but apparently all such students from a single school (or area) would constitute the sample to be used in the experiment. Such students, available at four specific hours during the school day, would be placed randomly in either the control or experimental group(s). (Usually, students so referred score well below average on standardized reading tests or are selected by teachers because of obvious difficulty in reading; relatively few are referred directly because of discipline problems.)

Procedures

During the school year four specific hours will be set aside for the experimental groups and the control groups (four of each): two morning hours and two afternoon hours, with groups alternating times so as to even out any effect thus occasioned. One week groups will meet three times, the next week two times, then three times—throughout the academic year. Thus either two or three days a week there would be eight classes involved in the experiment: four experimental and four control. Each of the eight classes would include from six to eight remedial students, the norm for the schools involved. The eight classes would be selected randomly, first by random assignment to experimental or control, then to particular class (at least insofar as scheduling permits).

The experimental classes would use the *Hooked on Books* materials, as earlier described. Each period, students would be required to read something and to write something in their journals, basically as the student chooses. Unless requested by a student, no direct instruction in reading would be given. Materials are to be discussed and book reports encouraged but not demanded. Journals would be checked to see that some writing had been accomplished, but no corrections would be made. The investigator uses the phrase, "Uninterrupted Sustained Silent Reading."

The control classes would be taught in the traditional manner, with emphasis placed on skills and with a variety of materials used: readers, workbooks, teacher-constructed materials.

All pupils in the experiment are to be tested at the beginning and end of the year with a standardized reading test.

Analysis of data

At year's end the difference between the mean scores of the experimental and control groups on the post-test would be analyzed using the analysis of variance or F-test (.05 level of confidence). The factor of time of day is to be considered as well as differences between experimental and control groups.

In addition, the investigator would provide (1) descriptive data on the post-test scores according to time of day, and (2) subtest scores (e.g., vocabulary, comprehension).

(Problems and limitations are mentioned by the investigator but not included here.)

Potential findings and consequences

Control groups might perform better; this would relate to a number of factors. Methods might show equally effective. The experimental group might do much better, or slightly better, than the control group in overall scores or in partial scores, or in a combination of these with time of day.

THE EFFECT OF TWO SEATING ARRANGEMENTS ON THE ARITHMETIC ACHIEVEMENT OF A SECOND-GRADE CLASS

There are many factors that can potentially affect achievement in the elementary school classroom. Could one of these factors be the physical arrangement of the chairs in the room? This is a study prepared by an elementary school teacher to determine whether achievement in second-grade arithmetic might be so affected.

The problem

It is the purpose of this study to determine the effect of two selected seating arrangements on the arithmetic achievement of a second-grade class. The two seating arrangements will be known as the "Table" arrangement *(TA)* and the "Double E" arrangement *(DE)*.

Need for the study

Eye contact is a prime factor in human communication. In the classroom, for demonstration-lecture lessons, a fan-shaped arrangement of chairs would provide optimum pupil-teacher eye contact, while for class discussions a circle would give the greatest degree of pupil-to-pupil and pupil-teacher eye contact. However, few classrooms are large enough to accommodate all pupils in such arrangements, and therefore modifications are to be preferred. Moreover, in the second grade the immaturity of the children make it difficult to move desks without complete disruption of the class. This study, therefore, will compare two fixed seating arrangements, one designed to provide maximum eye contact for discussion *(TA)* and one designed to provide maximum eye contact for demonstration-lecture lessons *(DE)*.

Hypothesis

The research hypothesis is that children seated according to the Double E arrangement for arithmetic instruction will demonstrate greater arithmetic achievement than those seated according to the Table arrangement.

Population and sample

The population for this study will be the second-grade classes in *X* Elementary School, present and future. From the population, two intact classes will be selected as a sample. These classes will be selected for two consecutive years.

Procedures

The study will be conducted over a two-year period using as subjects the second-grade classes taught by the experimenter. The proportion of boys and girls for the two years will be made the same by elimination of certain subjects from the study as necessary. The subjects remaining in the study will be paired by sex on the basis of IQ scores obtained from the pupils' cumulative folders. The mean IQ's of the two classes will be compared for equivalency using a *t*-test.

Previous arithmetic achievement will be measured by pretesting with the Metropolitan Achievement Test, Form A, within the first three weeks of school, and by comparing means on pretest results through a *t*-test. If the *t*-test reveals a statistically significant difference in means, one or more extreme scores will be eliminated from each group to provide equivalence.

The same teacher will teach both classes. The *TA* arrangement will be used the first year and the *DE* arrangement the second year.

Analysis of data

At the end of each academic year of the study, a second Metropolitan Achievement Test, Form C, will be administered. A *t*-test will be used to test the difference between means of the two classes.

The null hypothesis for the study is that the mean of the *DE* group will be equal to or less than the mean of the *TA* group. A one-tailed test will be used, and the null hypothesis will be rejected at the .05 level of significance.

Potential findings and consequences

If the data sustain the research hypothesis, the *DE* will be the preferred seating arrangement for the second grade. If no statistically significant difference is found at the .05 level, it can be concluded that either arrangement is satisfactory.

If the hypothesized difference in favor of *DE* does occur, it could mean that less distraction occurred in comparison to *TA* in which the children face each other directly.

Another possible implication might be that *DE* should be employed in other areas of the curriculum where whole-class teaching situations are used.

A STUDY OF THE EFFECTIVENESS OF THREE TEACHING ARRANGEMENTS OF A PLANETARIUM EXPERIENCE IN A FIFTH-GRADE ASTRONOMY UNIT

The planetarium is becoming much more accessible to the typical school-age child. There are currently over four hundred planetariums in the United States, many of which are part of the public school system. The author of this study is concerned with the effective use of the planetarium in teaching astronomy to fifth-graders.

The problem

The purpose of this study is to determine if the time placement of a visit to a planetarium during the course of a unit on astronomy will affect achievement during the unit.

Need for the study

The planetarium can be a very valuable resource to the teacher if it is properly used. One question of use is the proper time to take children to the planetarium for a visit. Should they be taken at the beginning of a unit on astronomy, at the end, or at some intermediate point? That is the question this study is designed to answer.

Hypothesis

Achievement scores of fifth-grade children on an astronomy unit will differ depending upon the time placement of a visit to a planetarium.

Population and sample

The population for this study shall be all present and future fifth-grade pupils in X school district. This population is contained in sixteen elementary schools with a total of twenty-five classes. Twelve of these classes shall be chosen at random to constitute the sample.

Procedures

The twelve classes selected for the study shall be randomly assigned to four experimental groups, three classes to a group. The treatment for the four groups shall differ as follows:

- *group A* shall have an astronomy unit with the use of textbook, available classroom facilities, and teacher's demonstration, but shall not visit the planetarium
- *group B* shall have an astronomy unit with a visit to the planetarium as an introduction to the unit. The classroom and text shall be used for the remaining six periods of the unit
- *group C* shall have an astronomy unit spending three periods in the classroom using the text, visiting the planetarium during the fourth period, and spending the three remaining periods in the classroom
- *group D* shall have an astronomy unit in the classroom for six periods and visit the planetarium during the seventh period as a conclusion to the unit

All astronomy units shall be taught by the researcher. All groups shall cover the same material with the same demonstrations and preparations. All groups shall have the same amount of time on the unit, seven forty-minute class periods.

Prior to the conduct of the experiment itself, the researcher will give a pretest on astronomy to all members of the sample. The post-test will be the science part of the Coordinated Scales of Attainment. As additional information, the researcher will obtain from the school records of each subject, a measure of their IQ and previous grades in science.

Analysis of data

Analysis will be made using standard computer programs. First a multiple regression analysis will be run using the post-test scores as a criterion and the three other measures as predictors. The best predictor will then be used as a covariate in an analysis of covariance on the post-test scores.

Potential findings and consequences

If the analysis of covariance shows a significant difference among groups, the null hypothesis will be rejected and the research hypothesis accepted. In the future, then, the best of the methods should be employed when using the planetarium as an education resource.

A STUDY OF THE PERCEIVED ROLE OF CERTAIN SCHOOL SUPERINTENDENTS IN PROFESSIONAL NEGOTIATIONS

As negotiations more and more become the mode of establishing such matters as teacher salaries, working conditions, benefits, and the like, the superintendent of schools inevitably becomes directly involved in either negotiations or their effects. This study attempts to determine, in one state, the perceptions that superintendents hold in regard to their role in negotiations. Is there a commonly held set of perceptions and expectations? Do superintendents create their own role? Are they key to or auxiliary to the negotiation process?

The problem

The purpose of the study is to identify the perceived role of school district superintendents of major districts within the state in regard to professional negotiations. Assumptions underlying the study include:

- questionnaire responses can enable the investigator to determine the perceptions held by superintendents
- clarification of perceptions will encourage further related investigations
- a useful purpose can be served by such clarification and categorizing
- the intended population of the study is large enough and representative enough to warrant generalization to all superintendents within the state concerned

Need for the study

Professional negotiations are increasingly a matter of concern to the top administration of school systems. Since the matter of bilateral negotiations is relatively new, the negotiating role of the superintendent is emerging, not fixed or customary. Hence information about the perceptions of superintendents in this matter is needed.

Hypothesis

There is a significant level of agreement as to definition and role expectations among superintendents in major districts in regard to negotiations. The null hypothesis is stated as no significant agreement.

Definition of key terms

- *professional negotiations.* Refers to a set of regulations, formal and subscribed to by the local education association and school board, that provides an orderly method for reaching agreement on certain matters and procedures and that provides channels for mediation and appeal.
- *superintendent.* The person hired by the local board to be its representative in the administration of the district's policies and programs.
- *local association.* The representative of the teachers and administrators in the local district for bargaining, etc.
- *major district.* One with ten thousand or more pupils.
- *second-class district.* One maintaining an accredited high school, one located within an incorporated city with at least three hundred population.

Population and sample

See remarks under "The problem."

Procedures

This descriptive survey is designed to obtain two types of information: (1) basic information on the superintendent filling out the questionnaire, and (2) ten questions, to be marked by the superintendent. The basic information asks for name, age, number of years in the superintendency, and total number of years as a superintendent. The ten questions deal with activities and dimensions relating to negotiations. The respondent is to mark these in one of four columns ranging from "never" to "always."

Copies of the questionnaire also will be mailed to ten randomly selected second-class school district superintendents as a pretest to determine validity of questions and proper phrasing and implications. Interviews then will follow these ten mailings and the return of the ten questionnaires in order to provide more detailed information about wording, implications, etc. of the questionnaire, which may then be revised if this is indicated. Next, about seventy superintendents of major districts will be sent the questionnaire, along with an explanatory letter and a self-addressed (investigator) return envelope.

Analysis of data

A mean score will be computed for responses to items in section two of the questionnaire, the ten questions referred to earlier. These responses will be ranked in order from the highest to lowest (total) mean scores according to preference or response level (e.g., "never," "always"). Following this treatment, the responses from part one (descriptive and personal data on superintendents) may be analyzed using chi-square procedures to accept or reject the null hypothesis. The investigator states that the chi-square will be applied to: age of respondent, number of years in present position, total years as a superintendent. The .05 level of confidence is stated. (The investigator then notes several weaknesses or potential hazards of the proposed study.)

Potential findings or implications

(1) The perceived role of superintendents varies among individuals or size of districts—or does not vary. (2) Factors about which information is obtained in the first part of the questionnaire determine, or seem to determine, perceptions, or fail to distinguish among respondents.

A COMPARISON BETWEEN TWO METHODS OF PHYSICAL EDUCATION IN THE DEVELOPMENT OF CARDIO-RESPIRATORY FITNESS

Many school principals and physical education supervisors tend to disparage a physical education program that consists mainly of playing games. They believe there should be more directed physical activities. Does it really make a difference?

The problem

The purpose of this study is to determine whether there will be a significant difference in the level of physical fitness as measured by cardio-respiratory efficiency between two groups of ninth-grade boys following two different programs of physical education. One group will play soccer; the other group will follow a program of calisthenics, circuit training, and games skills.

Need for the study

Boys display much more enthusiasm and expend much more effort when they play games than when they are participating in more formal physical exercises. This is an obvious advantage to the teacher. If the playing of a specific game such as soccer can be shown to be as effective in producing physical fitness as the more formal methods of physical education, then the teacher can feel justified in using games.

Hypothesis

Playing soccer will be as effective as calisthenics and circuit training in developing cardio-respiratory fitness as measured by the twelve-minute run.

Population and sample

The population will consist of ninth-grade boys in X Junior High School. From this population, two classes will be selected for the sample. This should provide between seventy and eighty boys for the study.

Procedures

The study will be conducted at the beginning of the academic year in the fall and continue for six weeks.

At the beginning of the study, all the boys in the two classes will do the twelve-minute run test. This test consists simply of running around a 440-yard track for twelve minutes. The boys are told to cover as much ground as possible in the allotted time. If they become too tired to run, they may walk. The teacher will stress that this is a maximum performance test.

Scoring of the test is done by the students. At the time of the test, the group will be divided into two equal groups and each boy will be paired with another boy in the opposite subgroup. One subgroup will run, while the other keeps track of the distance covered. Distance covered will be measured to the nearest one-sixteenth of a mile.

At the conclusion of the initial test, each boy will record the following information on a card:

- his name
- distance covered in twelve minutes
- whether he walks, cycles, or takes the bus to school
- whether he is a member of any of the school's athletic teams

The information on the cards will be used to assemble two matched groups for the experiment. Members of athletic teams will be eliminated from the study. The remaining students will be paired on the basis of initial test score and their mode of transit to school. The two groups will be compared by a *t*-test on the means and standard deviations of initial test results to demonstrate initial equivalency for the study. The groups will be randomly assigned to one or the other of the two programs of physical education.

The experiment will last for six weeks, with three class meetings each week. The soccer group will go outside and play soccer the entire period. The physical training group will stay in the gymnasium and carry out the following sequence of activities:

- five minutes of calisthenics
- twenty minutes in a twelve-station circuit
- twelve minutes of games skills practice and/or the playing of short games

Analysis of data

At the end of the experimental period, all students will be retested on the twelve-minute run. Mean scores of the two groups will be compared using a *t*-test. The null hypothesis will be rejected at the .10 level.

Potential findings and consequences

If playing soccer is shown to be as effective in developing physical fitness as the more formal activities, then playing soccer as a method of physical education can be justified. If soccer playing is not as effective, then it should be restricted to short periods after the circuit training part of the physical education program has been carried out.

A STUDY COMPARING THE RESULTS OF HEARING TESTS ADMINISTERED BY TRAINED SPEECH THERAPISTS AND BY SUPPORTIVE PERSONS

A part of the development of any profession is the need to decide which functions are to be performed only by the members of the profession and which might be performed by persons of lesser training. Since professional time is frequently at a premium, this can be an important problem. The proposer of this study is a speech therapist in the public schools who wishes to find out if lay personnel can be used to test children's hearing.

The problem

The purpose of this study is to determine if hearing tests administered by trained speech therapists will be more valid than hearing tests administered by supportive persons. Supportive persons are individuals, usually female, professionally untrained in speech pathology-audiology, who have available time and are willing to complete a three-day course of instruction in audiological testing.

Need for the study

Ideally, all hearing tests for children should be administered by a trained audiologist. In the past few years, however, the number of children to be tested has far outstripped the number of available audiologists. The speech therapist does not have sufficient time to do initial screening. Studies have demonstrated, however, the need for screening as many children as possible prior to the time of school entrance. Is it possible that subsequent to a brief period of instruction, nonprofessional personnel can be employed to do this type of screening?

Hypothesis

The hypothesis for this study is that there will be no difference in the validity of hearing tests administered by supportive persons and by speech therapists.

Population and sample

The population will consist of all children four to five years old who are resident in X County during the months of May and June. From this population, 360 children will be chosen on the basis of information available to the school district. Any children who are known to have emotional problems, to be autistic or retardates, or are considered to be too unsophisticated to respond during a hearing testing, will not be included in the sample. Any children who do not respond to instructions at the time of testing will also be excluded from the study.

Procedures

A letter describing the proposed study and requesting consent for participation for any child four to five years of age in the family will be mailed to all parents who have children in X County elementary schools. The first 360 responders, with the exclusions previously noted, will be notified that their child has been accepted for the study.

The testing team will consist of thirty-seven individuals—eighteen speech therapists, eighteen supportive persons, and one Ph.D. audiologist. The speech therapists must have completed professional work as prescribed by the American Speech and Hearing Association and must have had at least three years of clinical experience including the testing of hearing. The supportive persons will be chosen at random, two from each of the nine districts in the county.

The subjects' hearing acuity will be evaluated at five frequencies by air and four frequencies by bone in each ear. The testers will use five portable pure tone air and bone conduction audiometers that have been calibrated not more than two weeks prior to the study. (They may be recalibrated during the study if necessary.) The eighteen supportive persons will be given three days of instruction on the use of these instruments just prior to the beginning of the study.

A testing schedule will be set up for the 360 subjects. The parents will be notified of the time and place of testing. Twenty subjects will be scheduled each morning and twenty each afternoon for a period of nine days. All twenty will report at the same time.

As the subjects arrive at the testing site, they will be divided into four groups of five subjects each. Each therapist and each supportive person will be assigned to one group. Of the four groups, two will be tested first by the audiologist and then by the respective therapist or supportive person. The other two groups will be tested first by the therapist or the supportive person and then by the audiologist. This procedure will tend to minimize order effect.

Analysis of data

The measures obtained on each subject by the audiologist will serve as the criterion. Each subject will have eighteen thresholds, five by air conduction and four by bone conduction in each ear. Those thresholds reported by the speech therapists and by the supportive persons that do not differ by more than five decibels from the thresholds obtained by the audiologist will be considered "valid." All others will be considered "invalid." Chi-square analysis will be used to determine if there is a difference between the speech therapists and the supportive persons in the distribution of valid and invalid results.

Potential findings and consequences

If the null hypothesis is accepted, it may well be that the employment of supportive persons for the purpose of administering hearing evaluations would be valuable and justifiable procedure for public school districts. If the null hypothesis is rejected, it would seem that only the most highly trained persons should be involved in the identification of normal hearing and hearing loss in preschool children.

THE EFFECTS OF ISOLATION AS A MODIFIER OF DISRUPTIVE CLASSROOM BEHAVIOR

Control of the classroom is a persistent problem to teachers and, by effect, to students. What methods can be used to control effectively the students' behavior, to channel it and to modify it? Can the techniques of operant conditioning and its underlying assumptions be brought to bear?

The problem

Using operant-conditioning techniques, the investigator will attempt to determine whether or not disruptive classroom behavior can be lessened or modified by isolating, for a stated period, the student causing such a situation. Fourth-graders will be used in the study.

Need for the study

Any procedure that is acceptable, as normally defined, and feasible for reducing disruptive behavior in a classroom situation should abet the learning of members of the class. Various approaches toward reducing such behavior or eliminating it have been tried over time. This study attempts to determine if a procedure that has been used with small groups and individuals can be employed profitably in an ordinary classroom.

Hypothesis

The frequency of disruptive behavior in this situation will decrease during the phase period in which "time out" is in effect. The stated null hypothesis is that there will be no significant difference between frequencies of disruptive behavior occurring during the two phases: the "base-line" phase and the "time-out" phase (later described).

Definition of key terms

- *disruptive behavior.* Is that behavior which interferes with the constructive work of other students in the classroom.
- *time out.* An operant technique used to modify behavior; in this case, undesirable behavior. Specifically it prevents the student from obtaining reinforcement for his behavior by isolating him physically from the rest of the class.
- *operant technique.* A method of increasing the strength of a desirable (or approved) behavior or of decreasing the strength of undesirable behavior(s).

Population

An intact fourth-grade class whose teacher has experienced what he considers to be an excess amount of disruptive behavior and who would like to have his class participate in the *experiment* (investigator's term). This group is described by the investigator as a "sample."

Procedures

Key to the study is the use of a plywood cubicle three feet by three feet containing only a child's chair and a clock. The cubicle has no ceiling. It will occupy a space in the back of the classroom.

The experiment has two phases. First there is to be a twenty-day base-line phase during which the frequency of disruptive behavior is noted and recorded as it occurs in the classroom, without any change in setting (no cubicle). Second there is to be a twenty-day time-out phase with use of the contingency arrangement described above.

Before the first phase there will be a trial period of two hours on each of two days, during which the investigator and two other (psychology students) observers are present in the classroom in order to note behavior and record and compare same. This information will be discussed among observers and the classroom teacher. In this way disruptive behavior will be defined operationally for the purpose of the study. During the study, occasional discussions will occur when questionable (matters of definition) behavior is noted.

There will be an observer present at all times the class is in session during the base-line phase; just who will depend on observers' availability.

During both phases of the experiment, observers will record only that disruptive behavior which is indicated by reprimands given by the classroom teacher. During the base-line phase, observers will obtain practice in distinguishing between disruptive behavior and behavior that provokes a teacher reprimand but which is not defined as disruptive.

During the time-out phase, the only behavior to be recorded is that which causes a student to be sent to the time-out booth (cubicle). Moreover, it is the teacher who records such behavior during this phase of the experiment. The teacher now also must determine which reprimands are for disruptive behavior, not other behavior, and must send students so reprimanded immediately to the time-out/isolation booth. The teacher will wear a counter on his wrist and press the counter each time he isolates a student.

The time-out booth (cubicle) is not to be placed in the classroom until the morning of the first day of the time-out phase. The teacher will explain its presence and purpose to the class, emphasizing that the booth is to be used only for disruptive behavior manifestations, these being defined for the students as behaviors that interfere with the work of others in the classroom. The explanation and discussion will be direct and matter-of-fact, not emotional or dramatic.

The teacher will state that the treatment described benefits everyone.

When disruptive behavior occurs, the teacher will say to the student, "Five minutes time out." No discussion or argument will be allowed. No second chances. Any comment the student may want to make will be made to the teacher after the isolation period. The student will use the clock in the booth to time his period of isolation: five minutes. Self-timing is intended to reduce or avoid any reinforcement the student might get from the teacher by demanding special attention as a result of his disruptive behavior. The object of the isolation is to remove the student from the events and setting that produced the behavior or in which the behavior occurred.

Analysis of data

Data collected will include the frequency of disruptive behavior during the base-line phase and the time-out phase. Chi-square analysis (.05 confidence level) will be used to accept or reject the null hypothesis advanced.

(In noting possible weaknesses in his study, the investigator mentions several factors, and overlooks several other possible hazards. These are not included here, for the value of the exercise would be lessened by their inclusion.)

Potential findings and consequences

If the working (directed) hypothesis is accepted, an implication would be that time out is an effective device for controlling or decreasing disruptive behavior in the grade involved in the experiment. If rejected, the implication would be that this device is ineffective, at least in terms of the dimensions of the present study.

THE CORRELATION OF CERTAIN PERSONALITY TRAITS WITH ACADEMIC SUCCESS IN GENERAL EDUCATION AMONG ENTERING COLLEGE FRESHMEN

A current concern of researchers in higher education is the prediction of academic success from nonintellective factors. Certain investigators have claimed that personality factors may yield validity coefficients that are higher than those obtained using measures of aptitude. If this can be demonstrated to be the case, such factors could be used in place of the typical aptitude tests currently employed.

The problem

The purpose of this study is to determine if selected personality traits are correlated with academic success. Specifically, the problem is to determine the degree of relationship between the eighteen personality traits measured by the California Psychological Inventory (CPI) and grades received in General Education 121 (Humanities) by first-quarter freshmen at X College.

Need for the study

Colleges are always attempting to improve their predictions of academic success. Such predictions help them better to select students, to counsel them after acceptance, and to schedule them appropriately.

Hypothesis

The hypothesis for this study is that certain of the eighteen variables in the CPI will exhibit sufficient correlation with grades in General Education 121 that they could be combined in a multiple-regression equation to predict 75 percent of the variance in such grades.

Population and the sample

The population will consist of all freshmen enrolled in General Education 121, fall quarter (approximately 1,100 students). From these, 250 men and 250 women will be randomly selected for the sample. The last fifty of each sex so selected will be used only as alternates to take the place of "no shows" at registration time. The final sample will thus consist of two hundred men and two hundred women.

Procedures

The four hundred subjects will be divided into twenty groups of twenty-five students each. These groups will meet during the first week of fall quarter along with all other new freshmen, for advisement and orientation to the college. During one of these orientation sessions, the subjects will take the CPI.

A data card will be prepared for each subject. On this card will be his name, his student number, and the scores for each of the eighteen factors of the CPI. At the end of the quarter, the grade earned by the student in General Education 121 will be converted to a numerical value and added to the data card. These data will then be submitted to the computer center of the college for a standard multiple-regression analysis.

Analysis of data

The computer output will include an intercorrelation matrix for the CPI and the correlations of each of the eighteen variables with the grade in General Education 121. It will also include beta weights, regression coefficients, and their standard errors. The computer will also select the best possible combination of the eighteen factors for maximum correlation with the criterion.

Potential findings and consequences

It is possible that some combination of the eighteen variables of the CPI will account for 75 percent of the variance in the criterion. Even if it falls short of this, say only 50 percent of the variance, it will demonstrate that personality measures can be as effective in predicting academic success as the more conventional measures of academic aptitude.

A COMPARISON BETWEEN TWO METHODS OF TEACHING ALGEBRA —EXPOSITORY AND DISCOVERY— IN THE ELEVENTH GRADE IN A PRIVATE SCHOOL IN THAILAND

For all the research in ways to teach mathematics to high school students, there still are skeptics about anything but the traditional approaches. This investigator is, by implication, no such skeptic. She wants to determine, and demonstrate, that there are alternative ways to the traditional. It is interesting to note that she would conduct the study in a school system much different from those in the United States, but that the design of certain kinds of experiments is universal, even in school settings.

The problem

The investigator, an exchange student, is interested in comparing students' achievement as gained by exposure to one of two methods of teaching algebra: the traditional expository method (common in her school) and the "new math" or discovery approach.

Need for the study

The need for this study is the oldest in educational endeavor —the attempt to pinpoint and utilize an approach to a body of content that is most productive for student and teacher alike. In this situation certain institutional and cultural factors, as the investigator sees them, militate against attempting new approaches, although this is hardly a phenomenon singular to one country or area.

Definition of key terms

- *expository method.* Is a teacher-centered one, emphasizing telling, showing, justifying. It proceeds sequentially to additional examples and further steps.   ·
- *discovery method.* Is a student-centered one, emphasizing discovery, inference, induction, instances.
- *intelligence.* Refers to percentile scores obtained on a particular test with emphasis on the quantative portions of the standardized instrument (aptitude also enters the picture).
- *achievement.* Refers to the overall score obtained on certain teacher-made tests that relate to the content under discussion and to the skills and knowledge related thereto.

Hypotheses

First, there will be no significant difference in student performance or achievement as a result of one or the other method of instruction/learning (null hypothesis). Second, the interaction between the student's IQ and the two teaching methods will show no result in terms of achievement gains (null hypothesis).

Population and sample

The population is all eleventh-grade female students in science and mathematics at the private high school in which the investigator will teach. The sample consists of two intact classes chosen randomly from the schools' twelve math-science classes. One class, to be taught by the conventional method, will be the control group; the other class, to be taught by the discovery method, will be the experimental group. Each group will be composed of three subgroups differing by IQ—above average, average, below average; that is, the students in the two classes will be so categorized.

Procedures

Students in both groups are to use the same conventional text, one chosen by the school board and approved by the Ministry of Education. The teacher using the discovery method will have studied this approach in college. The other teacher, the one employing the expository approach, will have used this method for some time.

The students' algebra scores in the tenth grade, as derived from examinations conducted by the national testing committee, are to be used as the score for the pretest. To be sure the two groups do not differ significantly, the pretest scores will be checked using a t-test of significance (.10 confidence level).

The students in both groups will be given a standardized IQ test, one appropriate to the culture and content in question. Scores on this IQ test will be used to fit students in each class into the three IQ categories mentioned earlier.

At the end of each chapter of the text, students will be given a short identical test (stated as sixty minutes). Comparisons will be made between classes at the end of each such test using the chi-square at the .05 acceptance level.

The achievement test (main measurement item) will be a two-hour end-of-quarter examination conducted by the head mathematics teacher of the school; he will be assisted by senior mathematics teachers on the staff.

Analysis of data

The analysis of variance will be employed within a simple factorial design (two-way classification). The .05 level of confidence will be used to test the null hypotheses.

(The investigator then notes certain possible hazards or weaknesses in the study.)

Potential findings or implications

The potential findings discussed stem directly from the hypothesis—e.g., high IQ students may do better or worse under one method or another; all students may, on the average, do better or worse under a certain method; and so on. The investigator's intention, of course, is to determine the relative effectiveness of the two methods with the students in this particular school and then make recommendations about approach and grouping, assuming that a significant difference (or differences) occurs.

BIBLIOGRAPHY

Barnes, Fred P. *Research for the Practitioner in Education.* Washington, D.C.: National Education Association, 1964.

> A clearly written handbook dealing mainly with experimental research. It discusses not only possible designs but also methods of analysis appropriate to these designs.

Cook, David R. *A Guide to Educational Research.* Boston: Allyn and Bacon, Inc., 1965.

> This book not only presents the material usually found in a textbook on educational research, but also presents several representative studies from professional journals to illustrate the various methods of research.

Gage, N. L. *Handbook of Research on Teaching.* Chicago: Rand McNally and Company, 1963.

> This handbook might be called the bible of the educational researcher. Not only does it present extensive material on research methodology, but it also includes chapters reviewing the relevant research in many areas of the curriculum. It is a book with which every prospective educational researcher should be familiar, although not all parts will be easily understood by the beginner.

Good, Carter V. *Essentials of Educational Research.* New York: Appleton-Century-Crofts, 1966.

> An excellent introduction to research methodology for the beginning graduate student in education. It covers historical, descriptive, and experimental research. In addition, it tells how to write reports on the results of research.

Lindquist, E. F. *Statistical Analysis in Educational Research.* New York: Houghton Mifflin Company, 1940.

> This is one of the old classics in educational research. Some of the material given is now dated, but it is still difficult to beat Lindquist for clarity of presentation of abstract, statistical concepts.

Ray, William S. *An Introduction to Experimental Design.* New York: The Macmillan Company, 1960.

> This book was written primarily for students in psychology, but the treatment of the subject is sufficiently general that it can be studied profitably by most students. It is a book that is easy to understand because the author proceeds by small steps, always making clear the logic underlying each operation.

Wise, John E., S. J., *et al. Methods of Research in Education.* Boston: D. C. Heath and Company, 1967

> A clear presentation of hypothesis development, review of the literature, various methodologies, the use of statistics, etc. "Study Topics" are an aid to the reader.

In addition, the reader is referred to the bibliographies contained in the above listings, especially those published within the past few years. Also, any one of many self-study (programed) statistics texts dealing with contents discussed in the cases presented will provide basic background. The computer and its use in educational research provides a further area for study; here the most recent, understandable text the reader can acquire would most likely prove the best choice. Publishers' listings and college and university libraries (especially bibliographies) are sources to explore.

142   1   4145

71 72 73   7 6 5 4 3 2